The Hong Kong Sevens

A Book to Celebrate Ten Glorious Years of Rugby Sevens in Hong Kong

The Hong Kong Sevens
produced for
The Hong Kong Rugby Football Union
by
JMA Public Relations and Oracle Print Production
designed by
East West Promotional Marketing, Hong Kong.

Editorial Advisory Board: Glen Docherty, Jack Johnston,
Jeff Mann and John Mitchell

Photographers: Ray Cranbourn; Colin Elsey (Coloursport) London;
Peter Nance; Presse-Sports, Paris; David Wilkinson
and Edward Yu. (*)

Design Co-ordinator: Eric Chan

Project Co-ordinator: Marlene Lee

Published by
Arden Publishing Company Limited,
Suite 15A, 257 Gloucester Road,
Causeway Bay, Hong Kong

(*) HKRFU and the publishers wish to express their thanks to
Cathay Pacific Airways and the South China Morning Post for the
use of additional photographs from their respective archives.

Typeset by Oceanic Computerized Composing Ltd., Hong Kong
Colour separations by Rainbow Graphics Arts Co. Ltd., Hong Kong
Printed by Paramount Printing Co. Ltd., Hong Kong.

The Hong Kong Sevens

A Book to Celebrate Ten Glorious Years of Rugby Sevens in Hong Kong

Kevin Sinclair

An Arden Publication

Contents

It is with sorrow that we record the untimely death of Tokkie Smith on July 13, 1985. He will be sorely missed by all rugby enthusiasts.

Foreword

When Japan first received an invitation to play in a Seven-a-Side tournament in Hong Kong in 1976, it was a rather puzzling privilege. We were eager to come although we Rugby players in Japan did not know much about the event. Today, everyone in Rugby knows of the Hong Kong Sevens. But back in 1976, who could ever have believed that the weekend could have grown into such a famous, worldwide tournament. Every year since that first exciting competition the Sevens have shown healthy growth until they are now the best-known and most exciting event in the entire world of Rugby.

The original objective was to promote the game in our part of the world. I am sure that remains true today. It has certainly succeeded. Although none of the Asian countries have yet got to the finals of the Championship, the Tournament every year gives young players from the Far East the chance to mix with some of the most famous Rugby players in the world. These friendships formed both on and off the field have contributed greatly to enhancing the game in Asia and increasing the standard of play among young Asian followers of Rugby.

Those of us who are regular visitors to Hong Kong in the Spring have seen many dramatic, unforgettable scenes. Some games have been played almost underwater. Others have featured almost unbelievable running games. Every year, the Tournament leaves something to be remembered. The dinners after the games are also unique in the world of Rugby. I am sure there is no other place in the entire sporting universe where players from all over the world can get together after a weekend of endeavour on the field to eat, drink, sing and enjoy the real spirit of the game.

The Hong Kong Sevens are in good hands. They are being staged in the best spirit of the game of Rugby, a spirit of sportsmanship and friendly competition. I believe this book will help mark the 10th anniversary of the Hong Kong Sevens and will be but the first of many milestones in the long future of the history of the annual tournaments in Hong Kong.

Shiggy '987

Shiggy Konno OBE
Chairman, Japan Rugby Football Union
Secretary-General, Asian Rugby Football Union.

Birth

It was just another Monday morning in April, 1975. In his small, busy office amid the skyscrapers of the financial centre of Hong Kong, Chairman of the Hong Kong Rugby Football Union A.D.C. Smith was tackling piles of paperwork to do with his import-export business. The telephone rang and tobacco company executive Ian Gow asked what he was doing for lunch. "Nothing much", Smith said, and the pair arranged to meet in the nearby Hong Kong Club, an aging architectural monument to Victoriana where they often met to postmortem the weekend rugby they had watched. Over a pre-luncheon drink, Ian Gow leaned forward and quickly asked: "Have you ever thought of trying to organise an international rugby tournament in Hong Kong?" The question was put to the right person because ever since he was a teenager, Tokkie Smith had been doing little apart from playing rugby, thinking rugby, living rugby. As a boy in his native South Africa, he had played the game, as he had later in Rhodesia, in Britain and in the Far East. He had captained the Football Club team in Hong Kong, then the Colony side and at that time, in 1975, he was the Chairman of the Hongkong Rugby Football Union. But an international tournament? No, that was something that even the ambitious, rugby-mad Tokkie Smith had never envisaged.

Ian Gow explained what he had in the back of his mind. Teams would come from the leading rugby nations of the world to Hong Kong. They would meet over a period of several days on the playing fields of the territory in round-robin elimination series at the end of which the two surviving teams would clash in a game of champions. The idea immediately excited Tokkie Smith. For the rest of the lunch hour and well into the afternoon, the pair enthusiastically threw ideas back and forth. When they broke up, exhilarated by the possibilities that had arisen, they had much to ponder. What Ian Gow suggested was a vision with immense possibilities. It also held enormous challenge. The logistics were awesome. He visualised, in that first rough concept, teams from all over the world coming to Hong Kong for an international competition. The figures were difficult to grasp; at least 10 teams which meant 230 players and scores of officials and coaches. The matches would be spread over a period of days, meaning a huge financial and administrative committment to provide hotel accommodation and meals. It was an ambitious

Ian Gow, right Tokkie Smith, and Jock Campbell, left enjoy the atmosphere of the 1985 Sevens.

concept and one that gave Tokkie Smith much to think about. But Ian Gow had planted a seed in fertile ground.

The next time the men met, Tokkie Smith had a suggestion. The original idea was magnificent, he said. In scope and breadth, it was breathtaking. There had never before, in the entire history of rugby, been anything like it. But what troubled him, the Hong Kong Union Chairman said, was the huge cost and complexity of getting such an army of players and participants together. He had been mulling it over, Tokkie Smith told Ian Gow over a drink, and had come up with a slightly amended notion. What about if they had a Rugby Sevens tourney? This would hold several obvious advantages from a logistical point of view. It would immediately eliminate several of the greatest hurdles. First of all, a series involving Seven-a-Side teams would more than cut in half the number of people coming. Then, Sevens games were much shorter which meant that with games lasting 15 minutes each [22 minutes for the finals] the series could be completed in one day. This would in turn cut out a large part of a huge bill for hotel accommodation. And a full day of rugby in one venue would draw bigger crowds than a more extended session on a number of grounds.

Smith and Gow spent long exhausting but enjoyable hours discussing the idea. Then it was put to the Union which soon agreed in principle to the concept. At the end of April, 1975, the idea which had gained ardent support was put forward to the Rugby Football Union whose headquarters at Twickenham is in many ways the world Mecca of rugby lore. What Hong Kong proposed, what Rothmans generously wished to sponsor, was a unique and ambitious festival of sport. The proposal was to gather in Hong Kong

12 seven-a-side teams from Asian and Pacific nations. The enthusiasm for the fixture which was rapidly growing in Hong Kong was not shared by the administrators of the sport in Twickenham. Towards the end of May, 1975, a letter came back from England. It contained news that was a rude surprise for the Hong Kong rugby men.

Things were not as straightforward as they had seemed, said a letter from the R.F.U. It seemed there was a precedent involved. It all hinged on a resolution of the International Rugby Football Board and the tournament, as outlined, could not take place. The relevant resolution ruled that rugby unions at no level could take part in competitions or tournaments in which teams from several countries took part. Full details of sponsorship were also asked for by the R.F.U. As the International Board did not meet until March the following year, nothing could be decided by the top worldwide governing body of the sport until then. But indications were that the rule about multi-national meetings was outdated and would be revoked. Clinging to this hope, anxious to proceed with what was by now a consuming passion, the Hong Kong rugby lovers pressed ahead. Letters went back and forth from the Far East to Twickenham. Legal viewpoints were sought. Quiet discussions were held with enthusiasts and officials from overseas who passed through Hong Kong. The idea of the Sevens may have been a dream; it was by no means an impossible one.

By November, Hong Kong's own airline, Cathay Pacific, had joined the off-the-field team as an eager sponsor. Jock Campbell, then Cathay's promotion's manager and a man with a great love for life in general and sport in particular, was roped into the team. Managerial skill came from Cathay's Ronnie Poon and from banker and Union secretary Mike Pratt and others like Bob Gaff, all men with a drive that accepted willingly the burden of extra afterhours work demanded by Sevens organisation. Jock Campbell was to laughingly recall in later years those tempestuous early meetings. All was not plain sailing. Campbell remembers meetings at which tempers flared and fists crashed onto tables as details were being resolved with heated arguments. On one occasion, the normally-affable Tokkie Smith exploded at a committee meeting, bluntly told his co-organisers what they could do with the planned tournament and stormed furiously out of the room. Campbell ran down the corridor, told him that if he was to resign to do it formally... and the men went back to work in good humour. "Rugby committees can be quite volatile," Campbell was to recall a decade later. "Characters on the committee were diverse and this was reflected in the meetings. It was all very stimulating. And, looking back, enjoyable. Frequently, when controversial subjects were debated, it was like the clash of heads from opposing front rows and a fair amount of tough infighting in the loose mauls that followed." Ian Gow, Campbell remembers affectionately, was a

The Hong Kong Football Club stadium where the Sevens were held from 1976 until 1981.

The Sevens at the Hong Kong Football Club, in the evening amid the high buildings.

real professional when it came to promoting the right blend of teams to play in the original event.

As the planned kick-off date neared, the administrative problems with the international officials had been resolved and invitations had gone out. There were only four months in hand, precious little time to organise an initial international sports competition. But it was being handled in Hong Kong and the Colony's unofficial national battlecry — "No problem. Nothing is impossible." — was found to apply to sports events as well as to business deals. One by one, the problems were overcome. Little by little, things took shape. But plenty of unexpected difficulties kept on cropping up.

Where would 150 hotel beds be found? The Excelsior, long known as a sportsmen's venue, came to the party, thanks largely to the influence of that great rugby administrator and sportsman the late Vernon Roberts, then president of the Union and also head of Hong Kong Land, owners of the hotel. Cathay staff juggled tickets and air schedules. Hong Kong Rugby Union Secretary Mike Pratt spent every waking hour, and much of the night, trying to think of easy solutions to a thousand complex problems. Visas? Did Tongans need visas to come to Hong Kong? Would there be any dietary problems for players from Muslim countries? How would the Sri Lankans get from Colombo, one of the few Asian capitals to which Cathay did not fly, to Bangkok where they could catch a flight to Hong Kong?

As the teams began arriving towards the end of March, 1976, Ian Gow, Tokkie Smith, Mike Pratt, Jock Campbell and dozens of others were near mental exhaustion. "I felt as though I had tried to grab a ball from the middle of a scrum of Lions," Tokkie Smith said.

But the men who had struggled for a year and pushed frantically through the last four hectic months finally saw their dream come true. A referee's whistle blasted over the Hong Kong Football Club ground on March 28, 1976. A boot thudded into leather, a ball spun high into the air, the Australian Wallaroos and Korea's top Sevens players crashed in combat and the first match of the first Hong Kong Sevens spun and whirled into life. It was the start of more than a game of Rugby. Those in the stands saw a legend being born.

The Game Of Sevens

When the first Seven-a-Side competition was held in 1976, even some knowledgable Hong Kong Rugby enthusiasts were vague about the origins and forms of the more compact version of the game. They were soon to learn. In the years that followed, the annual glittering gathering in Hong Kong spread the love of the sprightly, fast-moving, swift-passing game all over the Rugby world. In Hong Kong itself, and elsewhere throughout the Far East and Pacific, Sevens has developed into a cult. To tell spectators about the game and to allow them to follow what was going on down on the field, the programme brochure included the rules of the competition. Put simply, these ruled that all matches would be seven minutes each way, with a minute interval. The final matches in the plate and main competition would be 10 minutes each way with two minute interval which, by that stage, would probably be a badly-needed respite for weary players. To ensure a fast-paced competition, rules about ties were outlined in detail. If scores were even, points for tries would outweigh points for penalties and drop goals. If there was still a tie, five kicks at goal by five different players on each team would decide the winners. If things were still even, they would be settled by tossing a coin. This sudden death system would eliminate delays in the run-up to the major games. In the finals, if there were ties at full time, play would be continued until one team scored. First to score would take all.

These rules went back to the rumoured origins of the Sevens. Just how and when the game started remains a matter for much conjecture late at night at the bar of the Hong Kong Football Club and similar gathering points around the world. One version, possibly too good to be true, holds that Sevens were born in Manchester around the turn of the century when a full-strength team of local butchers gathered for a match. Unfortunately for the butchers, their anti-social working hours meant they had a day off in the middle of the week when other rugby players were working. So they were a team looking for a game. With no opponents. The frustrated players decided that if they could find nobody else to play against, they would have to compete with each other. So they formed two seven-men teams, made the odd-man-out the referee [a jibe still heard — when the ref is out of earshot] and kicked off. So was born the game of rugby Seven-a-Side. The legend continues that at the end of the game, both teams had the same score. The reluctant referee, knowing his teamates, wished to avoid conflict, directed the side with

the ball to kick off anew. This they did and promptly scored. Just as promptly they walked off the field with the ball under the arm of the captain declaring themselves the winners. This incident is said to have not only given birth to the game of Sevens but also to have provided half the rules by which it is still played today.

Scots will dispute with Caledonian ferocity the claim that Sevens began south of the border. The facts are as unlikely as the Manchester scenario. The game can really be traced to the town butcher of Melrose in the Scottish Borders, a town where even today rugby is played with passion and Sevens with a particular flair. The local rugby football club membership was split in half when a new club was formed in nearby Galashiels in 1883. With neither Melrose nor Gala being able to field a full team, a keen player named Ned Haig, who really was the local butcher, came up with the idea of playing seven players a side. Yet another version of the tale is that the butchers in question hailed from the town of Hawick and it was only one butcher, at that, who started the game with some friends. It didn't even penetrate the Sassenach south until 1926, the Scots loyalists will aver, and it wasn't until after the war it went overseas in a major way. Wait a minute, others will cry. During World War II, Sevens was played during respites on the battlefields or behind the lines.

Ned Haig

No matter. What is known is that Cardiff won a tournament at Twickenham in 1939. Until 1976, the most famous Sevens tournaments were held along the Scottish border with England. Locals there would joke that since there were no more cattle rustling raids to lure the Scots south, they had to find some other excuse to go to England, so took up playing Seven-a-Side Rugby.

Ned Haig, by all accounts a man with a lively sense of humour as well as a passion for playing football, would probably chuckle at this theory and agree.

1976

The players who took to the Hong Kong Football Club pitch in 1976 had come under close scrutiny by Hong Kong players and followers long before they ran out onto the ground. Even before the kick-off in the initial game of the first Sevens, the event had caught the imagination of Hong Kong sportsmen. Takeo Tsuyama, the 5'10" Japanese scrumhalf from Meiji University had been the subject of much newspaper conjecture. The make-up of the Singaporean team [five of them were New Zealand expatriates] was dissected in print. The Fijians, after much soul-searching, had decided that rugby could co-exist with their Methodist beliefs which at home prevented them from playing on a Sunday. The speedy Sri Lankans, in tough training for months, arrived at Kai Tak airport penniless because of rigid currency restrictions back home and arrangements had to be made to feed them. The flying Thais were analysed in detail. The doughty Koreans were seen as a major menace. Local newspapers noted that New Zealand was being represented by a club team, the Cantabrians, which would be a side to watch with two full All Blacks and a string of top provincial players. The Wallaroos were said to be as bouncy as their name suggested. By the time Hong Kong selectors announced their choices on the eve of kick-off, there were FFW followers of any sport in Hong Kong who were not excited about the prospects of a major international competition being staged in the Colony.

The victorious Cantabrians — first winners of the Cup.

As excited as anyone was the rugby writer on the sports desk of the South China Morning Post. Most papers in Hong Kong had been paying close attention to the event as kick-off neared, and on the historic morning, the Post noted that it was the time for which all rugby enthusiasts in Asia had been waiting. Looking ahead to the Tournament, the paper noted the strengths of the leading contenders. But the writer made a point that was going to be made again and again and again in the decade to come... "The finalists —

Opposite page: A Fijian player about to be collared by two Wallaroos in the 1976 semi-final of the Cup.

who knows? They could be Fiji and the New Zealanders. Whoever they are and whatever the outcome, the signs are that this wonderful get-together will produce a memorable feast of sporting rugby." How right he was.

The venue for the rugby feast was also right. The Hong Kong Football Club, founded in 1886, is one of the Territory's most popular sports and recreational clubs. It was, appropriately, the home of the HKRFU, and the 12,000 capacity stadium in Happy Valley provided the sort of intimacy the crowds and players were to relish so much.

The Club's management had given their enthusiastic backing to the Organisers. Manager Jimmy Mair and his ground staff headed by Lo Kwok, made a valuable contribution to the event, setting the scene at the stadium and relieving the Organisers of at least some headaches.

Despite the formidable logistical problems which cropped up in the course of arranging the initial Tournament, the 12 teams that ran onto field in 1976 could arguably have been described as the cream of Asian and Pacific rugby. One teacher commented that the schoolchildren in the stands, a sizeable minority among the crowds, probably learned more over the weekend about the peoples and geography of the Far East from watching the teams play rugby than they would learn in a term in a classroom.

But geography lessons were far from the minds of the crowd when the first kick-off was greeted by a roar of approval. That cheer was to echo around the narrow arena of the Football Club stadium throughout the day. It was to resound from the surrounding hills and carry into club houses everywhere rugby is played around the world. It was perfect rugby weather. The sun smiled down on grass that was in prime condition, at least for the first few games, before furious sprigs churned up the ground as forwards drove into scrums and fleet backs were brought crashing down. For what the crowd was enjoying was a day jam packed with classic rugby; fast, running games with plenty of ball play, stunning passing, diving tries that carried players soaring over the line. From the press bench came an appreciative mutter as typewriters clattered out the news that would next day be headlines in Capetown and Suva, Christchurch, Pusan, Jakarta, Kobe and Colombo. "Champagne rugby," was a phrase often used by the scribes. And that summed up the style of play. It was bubbly, light, effervescent.

As possession is the name of the game is Sevens, little wonder both sides strive for the ball. A good example of this, from the 1976 Cup semi-final between the Fijians and the Wallaroos.

The first game set the style. The Wallaroos sent Korea down to defeat 21-4, and although the Australians deserved their convincing win it was not all as one-sided as the scores appeared. The Tongans gave the Aussies a short, sharp shock later in the day, pushing them to exertion. The green-and-gold jerseys were pushed back and back by the wiry, swift Tongans but Australia managed to clinch victory 12-10 and Tonga went on to the Plate later in the day to go down narrowly once more, this time 19-16 to Hong Kong. The home team had a mixed day, crashing to mighty Fiji 4-20, then scrambling back to beat Korea, Singapore and Tonga to win the Plate. The semi-finalists in the main competition were not surprising, the determined Japanese, the flying Fijians, the enthusiastic Wallaroos and the Cantabrians.

The best game of the day, postmortems concluded, was not the final championship game but the match between Fiji and Australia. It was a sparkling, exhilarating game, neck and neck, the ball flashing like a cannonball from player to player, snapping across and down the field as run after run saw two equal teams battle. First the sway of play was all in Fiji's favour and the first half ended with them holding a 10-0 lead. But after the break, the Australians came storming back, crackling, bursting, down the field. As the clock signalled full time, the scores were even, the game went into the sudden death zone — and tragedy struck for Fiji. There was a flurry, a swift, rough brawl, and a Fijian player was sent off. The Fijians fought on through one, then two periods of extra time. In the third period of extra time, Australia marked up another try and Fiji went to the sidelines to watch the grand final. It was worth watching. The Kiwis took to the field with confidence that was swiftly seen to be

justified. They got possession and kept it, relinquishing the ball only when they touched down tries and kicked goals. But once again, scores don't tell the full story and on the few occasions Australian players got their hands on the ball they ran with it to notch up two brilliant tries. The sheer clinical competence of the Kiwis took them to a 24-8 win, putting the Cantabrians firmly in the records book as the victors of the first Hong Kong Sevens.

First? Was there to be a repeat performance? Or would the players from all over the Asian continent and throughout the Pacific basin never meet again? In the minds of the spectators, there was no doubt, none whatsoever. The players felt likewise. It had been a splendid day, an occasion the like of which had seldom been seen before in the entire glorious history of rugby. But could it be repeated? Would the weary Organisers, those who had put so much effort into the exhaustive planning be prepared to sit down and go through it all again? Just as importantly, would the Sponsors feel it worth their while once more to come to the party with their generous backing without which the Sevens would be a mere pipedream?

In the emotive atmosphere of the after-match parties, there was not much doubt that there would be another Sevens. But when? And how many teams would be invited? And from where? These were questions that needed answers and as the old rugby songs were sung and as players from all nations celebrated enthusiastically as they waited to catch Cathay jets which would take them back home, Officials and Sponsors were quietly discussing the foundations they had laid and what permanent sporting structure they could realistically build on it.

Competitions — 1976

Cup Championship

Semi Final

WALLAROOS

Cup Final

WALLAROOS
14-10

FIJI

CANTABRIANS
24-8

JAPAN

CANTABRIANS
18-0

CANTABRIANS

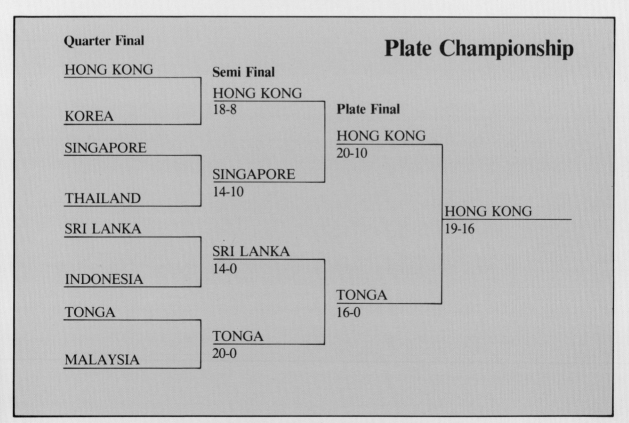

Plate Championship

Quarter Final

HONG KONG

Semi Final

HONG KONG
18-8

KOREA

SINGAPORE

Plate Final

HONG KONG
20-10

SINGAPORE
14-10

THAILAND

HONG KONG
19-16

SRI LANKA

SRI LANKA
14-0

INDONESIA

TONGA
16-0

TONGA

TONGA
20-0

MALAYSIA

Players — 1976

Cantabrians (New Zealand)
Ian Penrose
Lyn Davies
Ian Hurst
Duncan Hales
Scott Cartwright
Dave Thompson
Stuart Purdon
Ray Scott
Bruce McPhail

Fiji
S. T. Cavuilati
I. Makutu
T. Rabuli
Qele Ratu
V. Ratudrada
T. Rauluni
Josefa Rauto
T. J. Ravualala
Ilaitia Tuisese

Hong Kong
Bob Lloyd
Drew Lamont
Paul Davies
Jules Guerassimoff
Gus Cunningham
Ian Duncan
Paul Ogolter
Ian Kent
C. Collins

Indonesia
B. Huntley
M. Smith
K. Jackman
D. Cooke
D. Brownlee
D. Davies
Y. Magnon
S. Germa
D. Webster
M. Scrutton

Japan
Masaru Fujiwara
Manabu Sasada
Kyoichi Toyoyama
Takio Nishizuma
Yuji Matsuo
Fumio Ohyama
Hiroshi Hatamoto
Naoshi Kumagai
Takeo Tsuyama
Nobuyuki Takashima (M)

Korea
Lee Don-Ho
Kim Ki-Jung
Lee Bong-Sun
Lee Jong-Myung
Lee Chong-In
Lee Se-Jin
Uh Jin-Sun
Kang Won-Ku
Park Byoang-Cho
Son Doo-Ok (M)

Malaysia
Chalex Singh
Jagjit Cheong
Kaiyong Baharuddin
Hamid Abu
Hassan Nik
Hashim Taufik
Mustaffa Ahmad
Fuad Nubin
Jermain

Singapore
Hemi Williams
Takirua Tawhiao
M.M. Maaka
Brian Ralph
W.D. Tipene
Ray Cortty
Mohamed Taib
Teo Han Chua
Bohari Sarmani
N. B. Aitken (M)

Sri Lanka
Ronald Rodrigo
Shaan Ching
Jeffrey De Jong
Mohan Balasuriya
G. B. Gunadasa
Lanil M. Tennekoon
Maiya Gunasekera
Indratji Coomaraswamy
K. Rambukwelle (M)

Thailand
Rak Larn Sa-ard
Jirapan Davivongs
Chaiwat Kachasut
Banyong Pongpanich
Charuay Polprasert
Ruj Sankosik
Chatupon Punsoni
Vate Lenburi
Praccha Patachote
Wanchai Honghern

Tonga
Tui Halamaka
P. Latu
S. Vaihu
K. Mailangi
L. Ohi
H. Kaihiufahi
S. Ngaluafe
T. Alatini
M. Katoa

Wallaroos (Australia)
A. Gelling
S. Streeter
K. Bousfield
S. Mooney
A. Stewart
M. Hassell
P. Smith
J. Weekes
G. Thomas

ONWARDS... ???

Over-indulgent spectators were still shaking the cobwebs out of their heads in the week after the first Hong Kong Sevens when officials began seeking answers to some of the many questions the competition had raised. The first question was obvious; would there be another such event? The answer was equally simple from the point of view of everyone involved; yes, yes, yes! Indeed, on the night of the celebratory party following the games, there were already hints from the Sponsors that the day had been such a spectacular success that it would be repeated, possibly even expanded. Such were the views put forward on that exhilarating night by Ian Gow and Jock Campbell. These opinions were enthusiastically echoed by all. Invitations for Wales and England were mooted. As the happy, bawdy international sing-song was going on at the convention centre, officials were talking of plans for the future.

It did not take long for the immediate future to be decided. Yes, there would be a 1977 Seven-a-Side Rugby Championship. And, yes, it would be held in Hong Kong. At that stage of development, as there were to be for a few years to come, there were thoughts that the Tournament could develop into a moveable rugby feast, one year in this country, the next in another. But the logistics, the sponsorship, the efficient management structure, the proven ability to organise, manage and stage such an event were in Hong Kong. Planning for the 1977 fixture began while groundsmen at Happy Valley were still repairing the field from the severe bruising it had taken during the furious day of play.

One thing that ensured there would be at least a '77 tourney was the incredible public response. It came from enthusiasts in Hong Kong and from rugby lovers all over the world. The word of the amazing day spread rapidly and outcries about the future flowed into the office of the Hong Kong Union. As Tokkie Smith noted in letters of thanks to the Sponsors: "It was unquestionably the most colourful day of sport I have ever seen." Many compliments had come from those who would never otherwise have gone to see a game of rugby but who had been attracted by the carnival spirit and left convinced and dedicated rugby followers.

The Sevens was not the first bright plume in the collective hat of the Hong Kong Union. They had played host before to many touring teams, including a memorable match in 1975 by the mighty Welsh, and one year had organised the 3rd Asian Rugby Football Tournament. With its geographical location, its relaxed currency and immigration requirements, the abundance of good hotels, the efficient tourist infrastructure, the magic of the very name "Hong Kong" and the long history of rugby in the Colony, it was argued that nowhere else could compare as a site to hold an annual championship. Australia and New Zealand, perhaps, could host such a event. But from an Asian point of view, they were distant lands. Hong Kong, in the heart of the Far East, was the logical site. No matter what the future held, said Tokkie Smith, the Hong Kong Union was proud to have organised the event. It had put Hong Kong firmly on the international sporting map.

Rugby
In Hong Kong

On January 6, 1841, Captain Elliott, RN, dropped anchor off Hong Kong Island, raised the flag at what became known as Possession Point and declared it the latest colony of Queen Victoria. The chances are that some of the British opium traders who had for years been using the natural harbour as an anchorage had kicked a ball around ashore. Certainly, the new garrison, soon to be expanded following the First Opium War, played vigorous sports. The early rugby players of Hong Kong were probably a mixture of army officers, naval men and merchant cadets of the great British trading companies, the hongs, which made the newly-acquired British territory the base of their China trading. Certainly, yellowing newspapers in the Public Records Office in Hong Kong's Central District, not far from where the first business houses were sited, print accounts of early games.

Like most of the Colony's records, much of the written early history of rugby in Hong Kong was destroyed in World War II. In those hard days, anything that would burn was consumed in flames to cook the few scraps of food available. So the record books in which decades of games and players were written burnt beneath the cooking pots.

The 1985 Hong Kong Sevens Squad.

What is known, however, is that before World War I, the active Jock Macgregor was secretary of the Hong Kong Rugby Club. It was situated in Happy Valley not far from the Football Club of latter years and where the Hong Kong Sevens were to be held in their first successful years. In those days, of course, the hills surrounding the area were covered in trees, not skyscrapers. After-game refreshments centred on an old matshed, similar in material to the structures that had burned so disastrously at the adjacent race course

Opposite page: Hong Kong Football Club versus Royal Navy 1895.

in 1918 with a death toll of about 600. No such tragedy was to hit rugby players. The tiny expatriate population at the turn of the century included some fanatical rugby men. They formed a pattern that was to persist up to the present. It is a fortunate coincidence that one of the main sponsors of the Tournament today is the Hongkong and Shanghai Bank because their staff have since the early days of play in Hong Kong featured prominently in rugby photographs. The Bank provided one of the most fertile grounds of recruitment for early teams. So did the military. Not to mention the Royal Hong Kong Police whose teams have always been counted among the forefront of local clubs. Jardines, Swires, P & O, New Zealand Insurance... all the big companies were the source of players. From the 1920s until the foundation of the Peoples Republic of China in 1949, Hong Kong players made regular sorties north for inter-port games with Shanghai teams. There was great competition between the two great port cities.

After World War II, the garrison in Hongkong mushroomed. This provided, by Hong Kong standards, a huge manpower pool on which local selectors could draw. Local competition flourished. By 1951, the Colony/All Hongkong XV went to Japan. The manager/captain was Gerry Forsgate, later to serve as president of the Hong Kong Rugby Football Union for many years, a sportsman whose distinguished aid to sport was to gain wide recognition. The Japan trip was the first of many sporting tourneys, both away and at home. Whether playing the French Army in Saigon or hosting teams from England, Fiji or New Zealand, rugby in Hong Kong kept improving, both in popularity and prestige. By 1953, the Hong Kong Rugby Football Union was formed.

Club competition has always been the backbone of rugby in Hongkong. The Pentangular Tournament in the 1960s saw Police, Navy, Army, RAF and Club fight for supremacy. Visits to Hong Kong were made more frequently and these links, particularly with Japan and Thailand, led to Hong Kong's role in the founding of the Asian Rugby Football Union in 1967. Every year, to the delight of rugby fans and sports followers in general, an increasing number of teams from an ever-widening range of countries have headed to Hong Kong to play rugby. The start of the Sevens in 1976 and resulting interest among schools, not to mention the invaluable grassroots work of mini rugby organisers in taking fun rugby to boys, has helped to boost rugby in Hong Kong in the 1980s to spectacular levels.

1977

As soon as the Hong Kong Union announced the Sevens would be held again at Happy Valley in early 1977, players and officials in Asia and the Pacific hurled themselves into preparation. Nowhere was this more evident than on the lush tropical playing fields of Fiji. Rugby may have reached the Islands comparatively late, but the rangy islanders, twinkle-toed giants who loved to play in their barefeet and whose passes soared through the air with the grace, beauty and certainty of a South Pacific seagull, had taken to the game with a passion bordering on ecstasy. They came flying into Hong Kong in April 1977 with a determination that they would not this year come second to anyone. The hopes of the entire archipelago were with them; the local radio station had taken the unprecedented step of arranging a satellite link so the final games could be broadcast live back home in the Islands 7,000 miles away. They were confident their boys would make it to the finals. That confidence was soon to be proved extremely well justified.

Speculation on the attributes of the teams was a favoured way to pass the time in Hong Kong club houses as kick-off day on May 1 neared. It was Labour Day, some wags noted, and whoever won the championship would have to labour hard indeed to prise the cup from the grasp of the Kiwis. Many intended to give it a very good try, not least of all the Japanese who picked no fewer than eight national players to head for Hong Kong. Indonesia fielded what was a mini-United Nations side; its expatriate members had played in New Zealand, Australia, Uganda, France, Zambia. Tonga had five policemen in their squad and they arrived determined on vengeance for defeat the previous year. The Australian team was a bit of a mixed bag. Press experts analysed them as a group of highly talented individuals, but pointed out they had never before played as a team. Could they unite to pull together in the snappy, lightning game of Sevens, subtly different from the full strength, full length game?

A Tongan player is ready to scoop up the loose ball and just waiting for him to touch the ball is a Korean opponent ready to pounce in the 1977 Plate semi-final. The early pool games of the '77 Tournament provided plenty of excitement, much of it generated by the comparatively unknown talents of little-known Asian and Pacific teams. Now, thanks largely to the Sevens, they are renowned and respected in international rugby.

Ian Gow (left) and Jock Campbell congratulate Tonga, Plate winners in 1977.

When the Union organisers and the sponsors said the second Sevens would be held, it was announced the same 12 nations who had played the previous year would return to Happy Valley. In addition to the national sides from other countries, two would be represented by clubs, ISC Indonesia would take part as would the provincial Marlborough team from New Zealand. The Kiwis were not being under-rated by those in the know; Marlborough were the champions in the rugby-mad country and the side they were sending was a formidable one. They were picked to once again pluck victory from the rest of the pack.

The Hong Kong team, understandably, came under the most searching examination by the local rugby writers. The captain, Ian Duncan, was narrowly back on the field after nursing injuries. Other players, so gossip had it, were picked for their ability to display the quick, darting techniques so vital to Sevens success. Hong Kong coach Bob Lloyd had rich pickings through which to sort before plucking the final nine men who made up the squad. But Hong Kong was in for a shock, the sort of rude, unexpected reversal that is the very spice of exciting Sevens life. As expected, the home team won their first match against Malaysia 24-6. Just as expected was their subsequent 20-6 dismissal by Marlborough. But out of the blue came their trouncing by Korea, a 10-4 defeat that knocked them out of the competition. It wasn't that Hong Kong was not as good as the previous year,

Opposite page: A delighted Fijian captain collects the championship cup from Jock Campbell and a handshake from HKRFU president Vernon Roberts.

Cathay Pacific makes an unscheduled landing at the Football Club ground during a break in play in 1977. The unexpected arrival of an aerial visitor raised few eyebrows at a sporting event where, even in its second year, the unexpected was swiftly becoming the norm. The hang-glider captain scored a perfect goal-line landing between the posts.

players mused later as they replayed the games in the taproom of rugby bars. No, it was that the other sides had just got so much better. So they had. Especially the lesser-known teams like Sri Lanka, Thailand and Malaysia. Korea, too, came to the field with new skills added to their known determination, tactics the players admitted which had been honed by what they learned the previous year. These new approaches to the game made the Sevens a whole new equation. But no matter which way anyone added up the figures, the mathematics still made the Big Four the semi-finalists. The fight for top honours, it soon became apparent, would see the three South Pacific giants, the Kiwis, Aussies and Fijians, tussling with the brawny Japanese. As it turned out, the islanders from New Zealand and Fiji fought out the final game, but not before a display of boorish and shameful behaviour

marred the Australia-Fiji semi-final. A small but noisy group of spectators booed every move the Australians made. Nobody was more upset by this show of partisan and childish spitefulness than the Fijians. Many supporters in the stands were also quick to show their disgust and the two teams ignored the distractions to play on to a spectacular 15-4 win for the electrifying Islanders.

The final match began with a scorching pace. With a flick of the wrist, Fijian players sent the ball spiralling across the field. They darted, dived, ducked through the Kiwi line. They leapt and ran to a sparkling, brilliant victory and the crowd gave their darlings a roar that could almost have been heard in Suva without benefit of the satellite link. "The Harlem Globetrotters of Rugby," was how one sportswriter dubbed the fantastic, flying Fijians. "They're magicians," echoed another as eyes sought to follow the ball's incredible speed down the line. Admitted Ilaitia Tuisese, their giant captain in what must go down as one of the great understatements of sporting history: "Sevens is a running game. It seems we've got a flair for it."

After two years of brilliant rugby, there was still no permanence about the Hong Kong Sevens. Continuity remained in doubt. Was it to be a hand-to-mouth, year-by-year event or could something be done to ensure that annual Sevens competitions would always kick-off in Hong Kong? Nobody knew for certain, but at the "after Sevens" buffet and sing-song, some welcome hints were forthcoming. Cathay's Jock Campbell said exhuberantly: "It's here to stay." The press took this to mean that there would be a 1978 Tournament. Added Rothman's Ian Gow: "At this stage of the game, it's a definite starter." But, added Gow, a lot of planning had still to be done.

An elated Fiji side relax after their thrilling victory over New Zealand in the 1977 final.

Competitions — 1977

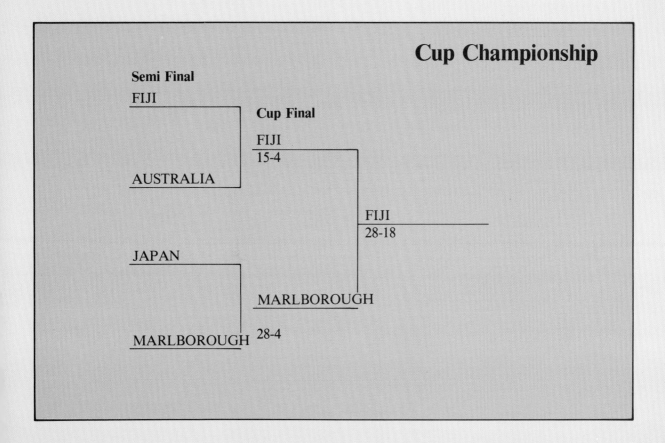

Cup Championship

Semi Final

FIJI

Cup Final

FIJI
15-4

AUSTRALIA

FIJI
28-18

JAPAN

MARLBOROUGH

MARLBOROUGH 28-4

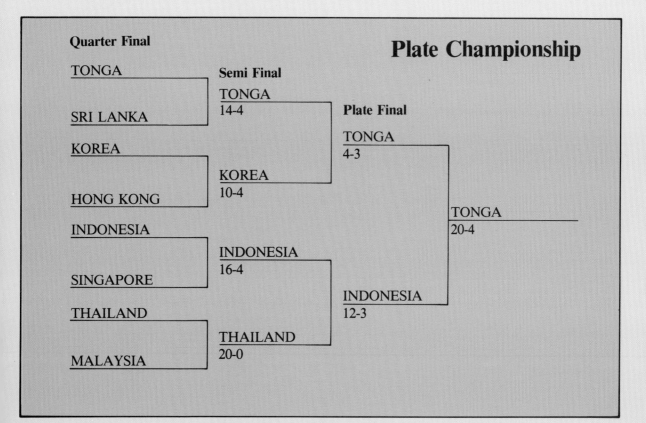

Plate Championship

Quarter Final

TONGA

Semi Final

TONGA
14-4

SRI LANKA

Plate Final

KOREA

TONGA
4-3

KOREA
10-4

HONG KONG

TONGA
20-4

INDONESIA

INDONESIA
16-4

SINGAPORE

INDONESIA
12-3

THAILAND

THAILAND
20-0

MALAYSIA

Players — 1977

Australia
Anthony Gelling
Paul McLean
Paul Smith
Jeffrey Weeks
K. Bousfield
Gregory Moloney
G. Noon
Anthony Shaw
William Ross

Fiji
Ilaitia Tuisese
Tui Cavuilati
Qele Ratu
Isimeli Batibasaga
Tevita Rabuli
Rupeni Ravonu
Vuata Narisia
Viliame Cegumalua
Robert Howard
Brian Wightman (M)

Hong Kong
Paul Ogolter
Norrie Rae
John Heptonstall
Ian Kent
Patrick Fegen
Brian Huddleston
Alistair Gumley
Drew Lamont
Ian Duncan
Bob Lloyd (M)

Indonesia
Murray Stuart
J. M. Smith
J. Cordony
C. A. Strudwick
C. R. Wokes
S. Rix
Michael Worrall
W.R.C. King

Japan
Masao Yoshida
Naoshi Kumagai
Manabu Sasada
Hirotaka Ujino
Ichiro Kobayashi
K. Toyama
Nobofumi Tanaka
Yuji Matsuo
Shigetaka Mori
Hisashi Yokoi (M)

Korea
Min Jun-Kee
Jung Hea-Keuk
Uh Jin-Sun
Ma Cho-Il
Park Byung-Cho
Lee Bong-Sun
Lee Jae-Moon
Park Chul-Kyu
Kang Wong-Kyu
Yun Won Ho (M)

Malaysia
Cheong Kai Yong
Zainuddin Mohamad
Ronnie N.T. Yeo
Mohamad Yatim
    Mohamad Zim
Boon Hoon Chee
Hamidon Abdullah
Ibrahim Osman
Arshad Ahmad
Mohamad Zainal Darus

New Zealand
Jim Love
Kerry Hodges
Brian Ford
Brian Dwyer
Jack Davie
Ala de Joux
Stephen Marfell
David Neal
Doug Saul (M)

Singapore
Peter Brookes
Duncan Richardson
Hemi Williams
Hamzah Bin Mohamad
Teo Han Chua
Brent Cook
Mike Richardson
Bruce Mataki
Andrew Chin
Kwok Kheun Choong
Richard Vanderput
Natahar Bava (M)

Thailand
Vate Lenburi
Narong Netcharoen
Chatupol Punsoni
Charuay Polprasert
Prajja Pattachote
Chaivat Kachasut
Van Lenburi
Vanchai Honghern
Mom Luang Chirapan
    Davivongs
Aroon Saenkosik (M)

Tonga
S. Matapule
P. Mapakaitalo
Hala Makaohi
Talilotu Ngaluafe
F. Valu
Valita Ma'ake
Sini Manu
Malakai Alatini
George Moleni (M)

Sri Lanka
Indrajit Coomaraswamy
Jeffery Ded Jong
Shaan Ching
Maiya Gunasekera
Jayaparkash Rudra
Jeffery Yu
Michael Muller
Gamimi Fernando (M)

The Nations

The rugby ball was taken to the corners of the earth in the haversacks of the British army. Later, businessmen were to spread the game in many lands. British immigrants who settled in Commonwealth countries grew up with rugby as part of their way of life. In other lands, rugby was played during the high tide of the British Empire and when the Union Jack came fluttering down the flagpoles as independence replaced colonial rule, the goalposts of rugby football grounds remained as one legacy of the past. Students from nations all over the world who went to Britain, Australia or New Zealand for schooling returned home not only with a grasp of technology, law, medicine or engineering, but also with books on rugby football. In the decade of its existence in Hong Kong, the nations represented at the Sevens learned their rugby lore from all these sources, and many others.

From its homeland in England, rugby travelled swiftly to the other three countries of Britain, taken home by boys going on holidays to Scotland, Ireland and Wales from the public schools of England where the game first gained popularity. Later, these same boys, as young men, were to take rugby to the ends of the earth where they played the game beneath the flag on which the sun never set. Today, rugby is a universal game. Nowhere is this more vividly evident than in the tiny city-state on the coast of

South China during the weekend of the annual Hong Kong Rugby Sevens.

ARGENTINA:

There is no doubt that the Pumas were popular in Hong Kong. They played bright, hard, attacking rugby with Latin dash and daring. They made welcome appearances in 1981 and 1982. Hopefully one day the big men from the pampas will put in a return performance on the field at Sookunpoo. The Pumas are the giants of South American rugby. The River Plate Rugby Union was founded in 1899 and although their homeland is a soccer-mad nation which has won the World Cup several times, rugby has always had a strong following. This has been particularly

Previous Page: Players from around the world — some straight off the pitch, others awaiting their first game — gather outside the players stand.

Below — The Hong Kong Hilton is the home of Sevens Rugby in Hong Kong every Spring. Players from around the world bring a sporting feeling to the hotel and in 1985 players from The Gulf felt right at home when they found a Middle East food festival was, by coincidence, being held there. HKRFU chairman Glen Docherty and Hilton general manager James Smith (left) chatted about the forthcoming festivities before the 1985 Sevens witnessed by a camel.

obvious among the large Anglo-Argentine community although the Sevens teams which came to Hong Kong featured players with names like Lorenzo, Perez and Logfreda. Not to mention Hugo Porta.

The Argentine Union comprises 56 clubs which battle through a six months season to select 16 provincial teams. In turn, national teams play sides from Brazil, Chile, Paraguay and Uraguay in the South American championships. Argentina has always won. Before the Falklands War, friendly visits were made regularly between Buenos Aires and Britain. Argentina also visited and hosted tours with national sides from all other leading rugby nations and for long has been one of the predominant nations in the rugby world.

AUSTRALIA:

It is possibly just as well that rugby is a minority sport in Australia. If the natural athletes of the continent all played rugby union instead of soccer, rugby league, Aussie Rules and other ball games, the Wallabies would possibly be eternal winners of every competition every played. As it is, they have stamped their sprig marks firmly on the fields of Hong Kong and are an inescapable part of the Sevens tradition. They have been to the heights of the Sevens, four times winners of the Cup, and taken to the depths by bad luck, being thrown out of the premier championship of the Tournament on the toss of a coin. And despite the traditional cheerful jeers of the crowd, the Aussies have in good times and bad alike upheld the highest convention of sport, rugby and the Sevens; they've always been great sports.

Rugby began early in Australia. British colonists took the game with them soon after it

became popularised in England. Officially, the first RF Union was formed in 1874. The ironic cry from the Sookunpoo stands is probably based on an historical inaccuracy. "C'mon the convicts!" is unlikely. The early reluctant sportsmen shipped to Australia in chains were probably soccer-playing Irishmen. Rugby playing English were more likely to be military officers guarding the convicts. Still, it's all taken in good heart. Whether Australia won or lost at the Sevens was not the most vital consideration, the executive director of their Union, John Dedrick, wrote before one Tournament. What did matter was that they brought to the stadium exciting, spectacular football that brought pleasure to spectators and players alike. They have certainly done that over the years. In grand fashion. "Our teams love visiting Hong Kong," Dedrick says, "they love the Sevens." Hong Kong loves them, too, although this might not be easy to believe when the crowd gives the Aussies the traditional boos as they take to the grass. There are strong rugby ties between the host clubs and the Down Under men in their distinctive gold and green; 1984 manager of the Wallabies was the popular Jules Guerassimoff who played for Hong Kong in the 1976 Sevens in which the home team won the Plate. With their particular flair and enormous ability, the Australians are one of the perpetual barriers over which any other team has to clamber if they have ambitions of winning the Sevens Cup.

BRUNEI:

There are lots of superlatives about Brunei. The smallest country, the newest nation, the richest population. There are similar adjectives to describe rugby in the country. The smallest number of players, the least-known, the most fanatical. Although assorted expatriate planters, businessmen and police officers were playing rugby in Brunei over the last five decades, it was only in 1976 that a small number of keen adherents asked the Rugby Football Union at Twickenham for membership. There were, recall old hands, three teams then playing in the country. The next year, they joined the Asian Rugby Football Union. In earlier years, British and Commonwealth military units dominated the game. But native Bruneians are noted as swift, fluid soccer players and furious exponents of the court game of takraw, which calls for instant response, a quick eye and fast reflexes. With encouragement from expatriate players, more clubs are springing up in the country, often linked to companies established there. Players who have newly-discovered the game are invariably wildly enthusiastic. When the Brunei team first came to the Sevens in 1979, all but one of the team were expatriates. The other was a Brunei-born Chinese. In recent years, in addition to the Welsh, Kiwis and Aussie expatriates, teams have included talented players with names like Batiang, Yong, Razak, Hussein and Hamid. A welcome indication that the game in Brunei is spreading its wings among the locals. This was particularly evident in 1984. The significance of a Brunei team at the Sevens that year, a team in which the majority of players were local Asians instead of expatriates, was made even more noteworthy because the new nation had come into official being only on January 1 that year. One of the strong points of the Sevens, as many have noted time after time, is that a country like Brunei with a scant 100 senior regular players can take to the field against the massed formidable presence of the All Blacks. They may not win, but it's an experience not to be missed. And the video tapes of the Tournament taken back to Negara Brunei Darussalam are an enormous incentive for young players to give of their best. One day, all going well, they too may be able to journey to Hong Kong.

CANADA:

When did rugby begin in Canada? According to faded records in British military archives, the answer goes back to the 1820s, soon after the game was born in Britain. Soldiers based in wintry garrisons played the game in the snow and men of the Royal Navy in Halifax and Esquimalt did likewise. The Montreal Football Club was founded in 1868 and inter-provincial games between Quebec and Ontario were common, and well-supported, in following decades. In the 1880s, rugby burst into life in British Columbia,

still the major stronghold, and until 1939 the game was played in many cities of the land. But then, like the grizzly bears, rugby went into a long hibernation. It was only in the past two decades that the game has rubbed the sleep out of its eyes and once again emerged in the vastness of the country as a major sport. Now, it is played in all 10 provinces with 10,000 men in 170 senior clubs playing regularly. The season is topsy-turvy; in most of the country the game is played between May and October because in the winter it is too cold and the ground is frozen. Only around Vancouver in southern British Columbia where the climate is relatively mild [by Canadian standards, that is; it does not freeze the ground iron-hard] is rugby played in the winter. Another time for Canadians to play rugby is in a weekend in March in Hong Kong. They have been doing that, with increasing success, since 1980 and their brisk style of open play, their sporting attitude and the affable friendliness of the big men from the prairies and the Rocky Mountains have won them many friends. During the 1970s, there was an explosion in interest in rugby throughout Canada. This followed the rebirth of the Canadian RF Union in 1965 after a long period of being dormant. To strengthen the game, inter-provincial championships were held for the Carling Bowl. Junior championships based on school and neighbourhood teams have also spread across the country. Mini-rugby is growing, a strong foundation on which to build future senior players.

In the last few years, rugby has boomed. In addition to regular trips to Hong Kong since 1980, Canadian teams have gone to Japan, Wales, England, France and Argentina. There is an annual, hard fought match with their southern neighbours. Every year, regulars in Hong Kong have noted how the Canadian teams at the Sevens have improved. If rugby keeps progressing this way in future, the world will see the emergence of another major power in the game.

ENGLAND:

The homeland of rugby has, sadly, never been represented in Hong Kong by a national Sevens side. This absence has been greatly compensated for by the appearance over the years of such worthy teams as the Public Schools Wanderers and the Barbarians. They brought to the field the best of British rugby traditions. The Wanderers, who came in 1984, were a formidable team and made it to the semi-finals. The Club's background is a worthy Chapter in English rugby. Formed in 1940 by Fleet Street journalist Charles Burton, the club during the war organised thousands of games for visiting servicemen from all over the British Commonwealth. Since then, the club has lived up to its wandering name, touring extensively in Europe, Africa and the Americas. Their motto — In Friendship We Flourish — was a most appropriate one to bring to Hong Kong where it could well have been adopted by the Sevens Tournament as a whole. The Barbarian Club, founded in the last century, was established with a similar sporting idea. W.P. Carpmael, captain of Blackheath Club, so admired some of the men with whom he clashed on the field that he wanted to play with them rather than against them. So a team of tourers, men with a lively sense of fun and who practised aggressive rugby, got together. In the near-century since then, they have roamed the world and when they first came to Hong Kong in 1981 on their first visit, they won the Sevens championship cup.

FIJI:

All the nice girls love a sailor, according to an old music hall ballad. Well, in Hong Kong in the Spring, every last rugby follower in the territory loves the Fijians. The amiable Island giants won the hearts of the crowd in 1976 when the first Sevens were played and they have been the darlings of the grandstands ever since. With good reason; their unfailing good humour, their sheer goodwill and good sportsmanship and the beaming smiles as broad as the Pacific Ocean

have endeared them to all. "They are the best ambassadors any country could ever have," is a comment that can be heard every year on the stands of Sookunpoo. They have proved that they are also about the best rugby players that any country could hope for.

There are an astonishing 600 rugby clubs in Fiji! Nobody can count the players. Every boy on the islands spends every spare moment kicking, running, tackling and passing on makeshift pitches beneath the coconut trees. And every one of these boys has in the forefront of his mind one blazing ambition — to carry the ball down the field in Sookunpoo. Like that other great Rugby nation of Wales on the other side of the world, the Fijians tend to go into battle carrying the cross and with Methodist hymns echoing on their lips. Also like the Welsh, they tend to win.

Rugby began in Fiji last century. The game that was played by British officers and later by the missionaries, was swiftly adopted by the ebullient Islanders. Fiji toured Tonga in 1924, starting a combative rugby tradition that has seen the two groups of islands struggle ever since for supremacy. In the '20s, New Zealand teams began touring Fiji regularly and in 1939 the Fijians went there. The visit stunned the Kiwis. It was unprecedented then and remains unequalled today. The Fijians won seven of their eight games and drew the other one. Since then, the All Blacks have looked to Fiji with vast respect. In 1964, the gentle giants went to Europe and Wales. The entire nation, developed an instant passion for the big, fast, friendly men, so different physically from the small, pale Welshmen but underneath it all so achingly similar in humanity and humour. The barefoot footballers, kicking almost into orbit and running like antelopes, were the toast of every tavern in the country. As they are in Hong Kong. There are a lot of adjectives descriptive of the Fijian open, lightning style of play. They've been called fast, furious, fantastic, flamboyant. Perhaps the best description comes from an imaginative newspaperman who described them in a headline as "Funtastique!" That's what they are, a mixture of fun and flair. And that's how they play their rugby.

FRANCE

The French Barbarians made their debut at Sookunpoo in 1984 with enormous Gallic flair and elan. They came to Hong Kong with an awesome reputation and an enviable record. Just the previous year the French Barbarians had gone to the other side of the Channel to take part in the centenary Sevens at Melrose. And in the Scottish rugby heartland where the Sevens were born, the flying Frenchmen beat the Scots at their own game. It was yet another pinnacle scaled by the keenest rugby nation in continental Europe.

There are many Anglo-Saxon customs which never take root in France. Rugby is an exception. Nobody seems to know just when the French started playing the game but between battles in the Crimean campaign British officers are known

to have introduced a strange new game to their counterparts from nearby French regiments. During breaks in the battles against the Tsarist armies, impromptu games were held, interrupted by such other events as the Charge of the Light Brigade and the storming of Sebastapol. Admirers of the modern aggressive style of French play may perceive still a hint of the battlefield where it is said to have been formed. Before their stunning victory in Melrose in 1983, French players had already built a reputation among the international rugby community. Their Union [formed in 1930] is a keen host of overseas tours. Virtually every rugby nation of note has been to their shores. In turn, the Frenchmen send

their squads abroad in increasing numbers. As the leading rugby power on the European mainland, France exerts enormous pressure for improvement on other rugby nations in the continent. They play regularly against Italy [a nation to watch, according to rugby prophets] and clash frequently with Rumania, a nation with close ethnic and language links with France and with a similar keen rugby tradition. It is often forgotten just how popular rugby is in France. Official records show no fewer than 1,700 clubs with 170,000 active players, the same number as New Zealand. It was the touring All Blacks against whom the French played their first international match in 1906, losing 38-8. They have more than made up for this since, having scored 86 victories over England, Scotland, Wales and Ireland. Not to mention handing out four defeats to the All Blacks, three to mighty South Africa and eight to Australia.

THE GULF:

The motto of the players from The Gulf could well be "None Keener." Few could be. The fanatics from the sands are mostly expatriates serving and working in the area and the winner of their annual competition is rewarded by being the club that sends a team to the Hong Kong Sevens. The competition is ferocious. Sides from Muscat, Bahrain and Dubai have come to Hong Kong. They have battled against vast odds. Muscat, for instance, selects its team from a pool consisting of a mere 35 players! To get into the finals is not only a huge credit, but borders on the miraculous. Gulf rugby began in 1968 in Dubai when keen expatriates expropriated temporarily a patch of desert, dubiously acquired some posts and awaited the cross-desert convoy of jeeps from the neighbouring sheikdom of Sharjah to provide the opposition. When they returned to the sandy rendezvous in 1970 for a rematch, they found electric pylons planted in the middle of the field. The Ruler of Dubai provided land which allowed rugby to continue and since then, the Gulf RF Union has amalgamated the effort of the Dubai Exiles, as the team is called, with players from other emirates and countries like Kuwait and Muscat into what must be one of the most active, if not the most unusual, rugby environment in the world. To get to play, the teams usually have to fly, the desert being rather short of roads. They are no strangers to Sevens. Possibly because of the sheer lack of players, the Gulf Sevens started in 1970, so when Bahrain arrived as the Gulf representatives for the first Hong Kong Sevens, they were possibly the most experienced team on the field. They had, after all, won the Gulf Sevens championship for the last three years. Gulf rugby is thriving, judging by the annual deluge of visitors wearing Arabic headgear who can be seen on the stands at Sookunpoo. The aim now is to spread the game from the expatriate communities in the emirates and nations that line the Gulf to local sportsmen.

INDONESIA:

Players representing the 13,700 islands that make up the sprawling archipelago nation describe themselves as ambassadors of the smallest, least-developed, poorest, most scraped-together rugby land in the world. The reason for this is simple; Indonesia has no traditional links with the game and simply, know nothing about it and don't play it. The men who head north from the rich islands come from three clubs; French oilmen from the fields of coastal Borneo, members of a club in Bandung accustomed to kicking-off on a field with a dangerous slope, and a crew of international Asian, Australasian and European expatriates who hold down executive jobs in Jakarta. In recent years, these three tiny, fragmented outposts of rugby in the vast country have tried to lure Indonesians onto the field to play the game. They have had little success. They have, however, marked up some surprising successes on the score boards at Happy Valley and Sookunpoo in the years they have been faithfully coming to Hong Kong to do their best in the Sevens. The mixed Australian, Japanese, New Zealand, Scots, French, Dutch and English players who comprise Indonesian teams are

sometimes strangers to each other until shortly before they run onto the field. But this volatile mix sometimes explodes into action that brings a shock to the big boys of rugby. Off the field, the players boast they resemble the Javanese White Rhinoceros. Once it was almost extinct. Now, like Indonesian rugby, it has a new lease of life. It also has a formidable thirst and the International Sports Club of Indonesia boasts that, when aroused, it can produce some of the finest drinkers ever seen. The same can be said for their nifty forwards; when aroused they are fine players.

The first rugby in Indonesia is said to have been played in the port city of Surabaya in East Java in 1946. The teams were made up of British sailors and soldiers engaged in the area in fierce fighting with nationalist forces and revolutionaries. It was not until 1972 that a collection of expatriates played a friendly game in Jakarta and the Indonesian RF Union was not formed until 1977. In recent years, spurred greatly by the annual exodus north to the Hong Kong Sevens, rugby in the country has flowered. Five clubs play regularly between themselves, against each other and with visiting teams from other Asian centres. The stress now lies in encouraging Indonesians to participate actively in the sport.

IRELAND:

When it was announced the Wolfhounds were to play in the 1984 Sevens, the big Irish community in Hong Kong were delighted. "And about time," they might well have said. The team that came was a microcosm of Irish rugby, a mixture of mustard-keen and swift youngsters and wise, experienced veterans. The Wolfhounds were late-comers to Irish rugby, as the Irish were to the Sevens. Formed in 1956 to help a new club, the Wolfhounds were aimed at being a mobile recruitment squad and rugby classroom. They meant to make attacking rugby popular by visiting country areas of Ireland to show youngsters what the game was all about. The local boys would have the chance to pit themselves against experienced internationals. Upgrading the game was the reason for the Wolfhounds roaming and they did it not only in Ireland but also during missions to Wales, England, Scotland, France and Spain.

The history of rugby in Ireland is a long and vivid one. The game was already being widely played when the Irish Football Union was formed in Dublin in 1871. But some Irish players, over post-game drinks, like to hint that rugby really began in the Emerald Isle centuries before William Webb Ellis made his fateful run at Rugby School. Whimsically, they claim the first rugby players were bold and burly Irishmen of old who played a rough-house game called 'Caid' which took them fighting from village to village across the land. Some opponents of latter-day Irish teams may well credit this theory.

Today, from school and club up to county level, 10,000 players regularly play rugby throughout the country and Irish teams take to the road to compete not only in the British Isles, but to wear the green jerseys as far afield as New Zealand, Australia and Europe.

JAPAN:

As in so many other fields, so it is in rugby; Japan is the Asian giant of the sport. Since 1899, when a Cambridge graduate named Edward Clark and a Tokyo enthusiast named Sinnosuke Tanaka introduced rugby to Keio University, the game has had a strong hold in the empire. From the home islands, Japanese players took the game to Taiwan, Korea and other countries. Every year since 1976, the Japanese have been putting up creditable performances at the Hong Kong Sevens and making a continuing impact on international rugby fields. Almost every university and major high school in Japan has its own rugby team;

there are more than 3,000 clubs in the nation. Companies field their own teams and by providing grounds overcome a problem of finding somewhere to play which has plagued rugby men in Japan for many years. There is no problem gaining supporters; more than 60,000 spectators turn up to cheer and watch the finals of major local competitions in Tokyo stadia.

Japan invites top overseas teams to the islands. The team loses, often by humiliating margins, but the Japanese rugby men grit their teeth, remember what lessons they were taught by their defeat and then issue more invitations to even more formidable opponents. Japanese coaches say the lack of massive weight in the forwards tells in their failures against such powerful teams as Australia and Wales. But they keep trying. Despite these defeats in the XVs tests with other nations, Japan has proved in Hong Kong that Sevens is a very different game. Concentrating on fast backs is the key to Japanese development both in XVs and Sevens, their coaches believe. The greatest handicap in rugby growth in Japan is the price of real estate. Once a promising young player leaves university, he finds it difficult to get a game. Sport Fields are not numerous. Only rich corporations can afford sufficient land for a playing field, so when young rugby men look for a job in Japan the company that has a rugby team is likely to be the one to which he applies for a position. The minimum price tag for land sufficient for a rugby ground in suburban Tokyo would be about HK$18 million. And there is the main reason that Japanese rugby has not proceeded as swiftly as it would otherwise have.

KOREA:

When Korean players gain possession of the ball, they go down the Sookunpoo field like an armoured division on the attack. The comparison is apt; rugby in Korea is centred within the armed forces and most of the teams which have come to Hong Kong to compete in every Sevens since 1976 has comprised a large percentage of soldiers. Rugby was taken to Korea by Japanese players when the peninsula nation was under the political domination of Tokyo. Today, although centred in the armed forces, rugby has also spread to the universities and returning students from overseas take back the rugby virus with them. Player strength in the country is estimated to be in the thousands and growing continually.

The performances put on by Korean teams in Hong Kong in the Hong Kong Sevens is vivid proof of how play against stiff opposition leads

For many of the players, the spare time in Hong Kong is a chance to visit the colony's famed duty free shops. Cameras are always a favourite buy — and are promptly put to use.

Welcome with a kiss for the arriving Fijians. A nice way to start a thrilling weekend of football.

to improvement. It also demonstrates amply the Korean drive to win, the determination to hang on at all costs and keep pressing on even when pinned down to their own goal line by a superior and more experienced team. With rugby spreading through the cities of Korea, there is no doubt that the iron-hard contingent from Seoul will be making major contributions to Sevens in future years. They have already spread their influence overseas; with armies of Korean construction workers, engineers and shipbuilders in the Middle East, the stocky men from the Land of the Morning Calm are now gathering expertise under the palm trees of Araby.

KWANG HUA-TAIPEI

The largest nation on earth in terms of population has enormous potential as a rugby giant. The lighter, swift Southerners are natural backs. The burly, solid Northern Chinese and Manchurians provide custom-made forwards in the same mould as the Koreans. Alas, rugby has made little headway in China, although a team of enthusiastic expatriates in the oil industry based in the southern city of Canton have in recent years been sweating in the steamy tropical heat of coastal China whipping up a league they hopefully call the China Rugby Union. The major rugby presence in China in recent years has arisen on the island of Taiwan and it was a Kwang Hua-Taipei team that first represented China in the 1984 Hong Kong Sevens.

Quirks of history took rugby to the island once known as Formosa. For a half-century it was under Japanese rule and in 1921 a student returning home to Taipei from school in Tokyo carried with him in his baggage an oddly shaped ball. Chen Chin-chung began to teach schoolboys to play the game and it spread throughout the island. In 1946, with Japanese rule ended, the Taiwanese Rugby Union was founded. The army took up the sport, giving it another impetus.

Today, rugby is big in Taiwan and getting bigger. The Taiwanese take to the game with their customary no-nonsense approach to life; referees and coaches are sent to training courses in Japan and Britain and Welshmen and Japanese are flown to Taipei to hold courses for local coaches. Since 1979, nations from around the Pacific rim have sent teams to the Pan Pacific RF Tournament which is held every second year. Taipei senir teams have played on grounds against national, provincial and club teams in countries from Japan to New Zealand, Bahrain to Tonga. In Taiwan, more than 5,000 players in 26 clubs compete regularly. The Taiwanese plan to send a national team to Australia and New Zealand.

This vigorous background holds great promise for the future of rugby on the island. And if the sporting fever spreads across the Straits of Taiwan to infect a billion Chinese in the mainland, the entire map of world rugby will have to be swiftly redrawn.

MALAYSIA:

Every year since 1954, Malaysian teams have been competing against neighbouring Thailand for one of the lesser-known trophies in the rugby world, the Vajiralongkorn Cup. Donated by the Thai King and named after the Crown Prince, the Cup is the symbol of healthy bilateral competition between the rugby players of two keen nations. It is just one of the many international links that Malaysia has with the rest of the rugby world. Well-established in colonial days, rugby in the country is now bursting into a new, vibrant life. Expatriates were playing the game last century, but today it is Malays, Chinese, Indians, Eurasians and the other races of the country who take to the field in a bewildering series of competitions, tournaments and cup fixtures. There are Under-23 tournaments and 10-a-side contests. A national Sevens competition has been started to select players to come to Hong Kong. There is rugby in schools, in clubs, at universities and in the armed forces. There are two level competitions at state levels, international tournaments, under-15 contests and inter-club games. When more outings are needed, Malaysia plays host to visitors from many other rugby nations or sends teams overseas to compete. Rugby is alive and well in Malaysia — and growing every year.

NEW ZEALAND:

There is an old saying that rugby is the religion of New Zealand. Not true. It's more important than that. In every tiny farming hamlet the length of the country, in every town and city park, groups of boys can be seen any day of the week kicking a rugby ball. These boys have one ambition; when they grow up into huge hookers, hulking props, fiery half-backs or fleet wingers they want to wear the striking jet black jersey with the silver fern that has crushed and dazzled opposing teams on virtually every major rugby ground in the world. They want to become All Blacks. It is no accident that New Zealand is one of the true superpowers of the rugby world. Generations of Kiwis have taken their first uncertain steps across a suburban back lawn or on a country farm to kick a ball under the discerning eye of brothers, fathers and grandfathers who all played the game. Rugby is not just a way of life in New Zealand; to a large proportion of the population it is what life is all about.

Rugby began early in the South Pacific. Officers of the huge British army that went to fight the Maori Wars of the 1860s took with them rugby balls as well as rifles. The Maoris were soon to display a frightening aptitude with both and it is no coincidence that when touring All Black teams run onto rugby fields around the world they preceed their endeavours on the field with a spirited Haka, the Maori war dance. By 1892, the New Zealand RF Union was founded.

Clubs had already sprouted in provincial centres throughout the country and can trace their heritage back even further. In many farming areas, towns consisted of a pub, a church, a school and a set of goal posts. It was from just such small settlements that some of the players originated who came to Hong Kong as the Cantabrian team to take part in the first Sevens in 1976. They won. Other club teams over later years were less successful and after a dismal showing by an Auckland team in 1981, no invitation was issued for the 1982 Tournament but in 1983 the All Blacks sent a national side which reached the quarter finals and in 1984 they lost in the championship match to their old friends and opponents from Fiji. The hard-driving, massive forwards' power that drove the All Black to victory after stunning victory over the years, conquering at one time or other every major rugby power and in eternal see-saw conflict with that other rugby colossus, South Africa, is not the same advantage in Sevens as it is in the big XVs game. Sevens in New Zealand was only recognised on a national basis in 1975. Although masters of the XVs, the All Blacks conceded when they came to Hong Kong as a national team in 1983 that they had a lot to learn about the faster, running tactics of Sevens. There is no school to rival the Sookunpoo stadium, as they demonstrated the next year when they came back to motor their way into the finals.

PAPUA NEW GUINEA:

When the Hong Kong Sevens were first expanded from the original 12 sides to 16 teams in 1978, one of the newcomers were the engaging Puk Puks. That means Crocodile in Pidgin and that is the language that the Papua New Guinea team used on the field. It is the tongue that unifies the people of a nation that speaks 700 different languages and dialects. Talking to each other is only the start of the problems for keen rugby players in the country. It is a nation dedicated to rugby league, probably because of the long Australian colonial presence, and more than 50,000 players from 1,000 clubs play league every weekend. Many thousands more play soccer. In contrast, only about 360 players in eight clubs centred around the capital of Port Moresby play Union. The rugby men from Moresby have to make great personal sacrifices to raise funds to send themselves overseas for the combat in competition that is needed to raise their standards of play. Sometimes, they must ask themselves if the effort and expense is worthwhile; in one match they lost to Fiji 96-0. But still they try.

Thanks in great part to the annual overseas odyssey to Hong Kong, rugby is making something of a comeback in Papua New Guinea. Another boost comes from an increasing number of New Zealand expatriates working there; in addition to technical skills, they have also imported their natural love of rugby. When the Puk Puks came in 1978, they were not sure, exactly, what Seven-a-Side rugby was. But they saw a couple of practice sessions of other contenders, then went out for a brief training session of their own. They then took to the field and stunned every last person in the crowded stadium by beating the Japanese. Nobody, even the Japanese players, were as surprised as the Puk Puks. "The mighty minnows," they were promptly dubbed. All the world loves a gallant loser, and the Hong Kong crowd have long adored the friendly Pacific men whose jerseys wear an emblem featuring a hungry croc. Nothing could be further from their smiling nature.

SCOTLAND:

A team from the Scottish Border Club is as close as one can come to having a national Scotland side; it is not uncommon for two thirds of a Scottish XV to come from the border lands. Not only is it the heartland of Scottish rugby, it is also the territory in which Sevens were born and where they still flourish mightily. The Borderers came to Hong Kong knowing well the differences between XVs rugby and the faster, looser Sevens. So they should; the first Sevens tournament was played at the Greenyards at Melrose in 1883. The invitation to them to play in the '82 tournament in Hong Kong came as a great honour, the Borderers' officials said. It was an honour to have them, the hosts countered. When they got to Hong Kong, Borderers sometimes had to explain to players from other lands that they really did not quite exist. Not physically. There was no clubhouse, no ground, no players. They were just a bunch who got together from seven club sides in southern Scotland to play rugby. Their tie was almost as confusing as the explanation. It contained the green of Hawick, royal blue of Jedforest, navy blue of Selkirk, yellow and black of Melrose, scarlet of Langholm, maroon of Gala, black and white of Kelso... But despite this confusing non-existence, the Borderers went on to explain, they had since 1953 won 11 championships outright and shared 10 more. "I see," said a baffled Thai after hearing this story. "Well, have a drink, anyway." The Lion Rampant flag of Scotland was also proudly borne to Hong Kong by the Co-optimists team, also exponents of the North British running rugby style. The famous invitation-only club was founded in 1924 with the aim of making rugby popular in areas where other ball games predominated. The name? To popularise rugby, the name was taken from that used by a noted musical hall act. With no ground, no membership fee and only two fixed annual games, the Co-optimists until 1982 had a unique tradition of never meeting together for a training session before they left the shores of Scotland to play a game abroad. This did not seem to hamper them greatly when they first came to Hong Kong in 1980 and they fought their way up to the finals only to be downed in the last match of the competition by the mighty Fijians.

SINGAPORE:

The history of rugby in Singapore is a microcosm of developments in many countries in the Far East over the past century. When a rugby ball was first kicked around the playing fields of the island state last century, it was then a British protectorate. Those doing the kicking and running where British servicemen or expatriates working with the mighty European banks, trading houses or shipping companies engaged in Asian trade. Even in the first years of the Sevens, a large percentage of the Singaporean team were foreigners, usually New Zealand soldiers based on the Island. But in recent years, the national team have been Island-born and a glance at any of the portraits of players in the annual Sevens programmes shows how the players reflect the rich racial diversity of the nation. Sikhs, Chinese, Malays, Bengalis... they are now the men who wear the Singaporean jerseys.

Sailors and soldiers played rugby in Singapore last century when it was a great British military base. Unofficial games were staged by members of different firms which fielded teams of different sizes in friendly, informal and very fluid matches. It was not until 1922 that rugby began on a more formal basis with competition for the HMS Malaya cup, donated by the Royal Navy. Until 1959 and the coming of independence, rugby was mostly an expatriate sport. Two trends changed this picture. The British forces pulled out of the East and at the same time local executives took over the chairs of foreigners in many leading companies. With fewer hefty foreigners on whom to draw, selectors of the Singapore Union picked promising locals to fill the gaps. Because most players are considerably lighter than their heavyweight opponents from Australia, Britain, Fiji and Samoa, Singapore rugby coaches and officials have stressed the need for their lighter, faster players to get the ball, pass it swiftly and run with it as fast as possible. This needs 150 percent fitness, Singapore officials tell their players. That fitness is what has made the Singapore team one of the most successful in the Asian region.

SOLOMON ISLANDS:

There is not a great deal to do in Bellona. Only 800 Polynesians live on the tropical speck 200 miles south of the main Solomons island of Guadalcanal. What they do most of the time between farming and fishing is play rugby. And they do that very well indeed. The Bellona team play so spectacularly that in 1982 they won the Solomons Island Seven-a-Side tournament. And when the country was invited to send a team to Hong Kong in 1983, no fewer than three of the players came from the remote islet. Most of the nation are Melanesians, but like the Bellona Islanders they share a taste for rugby. Geographically isolated from the mainstream of the sport, they are heavily influenced by their South Pacific neighbours and play a fast, running game in which maximum use is made of possession. This is vital in playing against such powerful teams as visiting Australians from whom it is difficult to get the ball. The 1983 visit to Hong Kong was an eye-opener in more ways than one. The Solomons entire population is less than that of some larger Hong Kong public housing estates. For many of the players, it was their first trip out of the Solomons and their first match against top world international players. They acquitted themselves well. They were put down 26-0 by Australia, annihilated 40-0 by Japan but managed to beat Malaysia 20-4. This victory took them to the semi-finals of the Plate where they, surprisingly, beat Thailand before being knocked out of competition by Korea. It was a creditable performance by the tiny newcomers to the big time.

Cut off from international competition, rugby has grown internally. More than 20 clubs compete in the capital of Honiara and other teams are scattered over outlying islands. In Bellona, they can only play each other. Rugby is a new sport in the Solomons. For many years it was discouraged by colonial administrators for a bizarre reason. Because malaria was once endemic on the islands, many of the young men had enlarged livers. It

was feared that taking part in rough-and-tumble rugby matches would swamp the one hospital and handful of clinics on the islands with patients suffering ruptured spleens. So it was not until the 1960s that the game got a grip. With the incidence of malaria dropping, there are no longer such an excessive number of large spleens among young Solomon Islanders. But those who have seen their young men on the field at Sookunpoo will tell you that the Solomons rugby men have big hearts.

SRI LANKA:

Rugby balls have been kicked around the military cantonments and government compounds of Sri Lanka for more than a century. But until independence it was mostly a game for expatriates. But as long ago as 1891, indigenous peoples were playing the game and it has long been favoured by a minority of sportsmen. In recent years, however, rugby has been making a resurgence in the hill towns of the country and clubs are starting among schools. While still mainly centred around Colombo, inter-club competitions are being played in other centres. As it does everywhere, the future of Sri Lankan rugby lies in the schools and a strong boost to the game was given by participation in the Asian Schools RF tournament. This gave young Sri Lankan players the rare and welcome chance to take to the field against experienced youngsters from other lands. Getting them onto the field even younger is the task set those who organise mini rugby on the island. More than 40 teams now take part on a regular basis and as these promising young players grow up, they will be laying a foundation for improved standards of play in the future. Schools Seven-a-Side tournaments are also held, part of the drive to get players ready to take part in what Sri Lankan officials and players see as the premier event of the year, the annual journey to the Hong Kong Sevens. The Sevens, say officials from Colombo, have given the greatest impetus in recent years to the cause of Sri Lankan rugby.

THAILAND:

Potential rugby players in much of Thailand have a major problem. There are few sportsgrounds. With only about 1,500 players in the Kingdom, it is a wonder that Thailand every year manages to get together a team to put on the field at Sookunpoo. But manage they do and although they are overwhelmed by the well-disciplined might of the major rugby nations, the Thais win the admiration of the crowd by their attitude; try, try and try again.

Top rugby in Thailand is more or less restricted to the universities and a few rugby clubs, mainly expatriate, in Bangkok. The other venue for rugby players is the military where the sport has a lengthy tradition. The Hong Kong Sevens have been a big boon to Thai rugby; the annual invitation to the Tournament is a magnet that encourages young players to do their best. But, lament Thai officials, trying to promote the game is difficult. "Without grounds, we are like gypsies trying to find somewhere to play," complains one leading Bangkok rugby organiser. The record is not all grim. In Sevens competitions, they have defeated Malaysia [1977] and almost brought down the home team in 1978. Rugby in Thailand was introduced by expatriate British businessmen in the 1920s. Thai onlookers at the Royal Bangkok Sports Club thought it hugely amusing to watch largish gentlemen put their arms around each other, bend over and butt each other like elephants in the teak forests to gain possession of a strangely shaped ball. This amusement turned to emulation after the Thai Rugby Union was formed in 1938 and the game passed into Bangkok universities, Military establishments and was taken up with enthusiasm by members of the ruling classes who had returned home from Britain with degrees from Oxbridge and a love of rugby. As a founder member of the Asian Rugby Football Union, Thai officials promote rugby in the Kingdom in imaginative ways. There is an Asia-wide schools tournament and club competition and interest in the game grows yearly.

TONGA:

Seven-a-Side rugby began in Tonga for reasons similar to the game becoming popularised elsewhere. Coaches used it as a get-fit gimmick to smarten-up players before the start of the major XVs season. Today, on Tonga as elsewhere, Sevens is being taken a lot more seriously. When Tongan officials received an invitation to come to the first Sevens in 1976, they had been playing the game in a light-hearted manner for six seasons. The invitation was grasped eagerly and the Tongans have been popular players ever since. Every year, the Tongan players and officials swear, they learn a little more. Every year, they come back stronger. In 1977, they grasped the Plate. The rich history of rugby in Tonga goes back to the start of the century. But it really began in 1924 with the first international between Tonga and Fiji. The South Pacific cousins have been locked in battle on the rugby field ever since. But there have been more extensive links with regular exchanges between other island neighbours such as Western Samoa and increasingly with Australia and New Zealand. Tonga has toured New Zealand and Britain and hosted numerous visiting teams. But it is the Hong Kong Sevens that are now the biggest event on the Island rugby calendar. "It's our annual migration," say officials. There are more than 3,000 active players in the 70 clubs in Tonga and about 18,000 people, roughly a fifth of the entire national population, can squeeze into Teufaiva Park to see an international game. With rugby very active at club level, Tonga is building a new generation of players to follow in the sprig-marks of the men who blazed the trail to Hong Kong a decade ago.

UNITED STATES:

By almost any yardstick, America has everything most countries could desire. In one way, however, it is a deprived area. They do not have a rich tradition of rugby. America's own baffling variety of football may very well be fascinating and enjoyable for those who understand it. For rugby lovers, however, it can't compete with the real thing. The USA Union was formed only in 1975. Before that, the game was spreading through the country like an unknown underground cult; nobody seemed to know just how many people were playing it, where. But many believed rugby was more widely played than anyone realised. It soon became apparent that this was so, that rugby was being played in

many areas of the country by a large number of people. With a national body formed to help foster active local clubs scattered throughout the country, US rugby soon found its feet. The national team, the Eagles, played Australia and France in America in 1976. The next year they went to England and in 1980 to Wales. In 1981, they came to Hong Kong for the Sevens. With the vast reservoir of sporting talent in the United States, it was not surprising that the team the Eagles saw clapped onto the field comprised some top athletes. It was obvious, however, that they had a lot to learn about Sevens. In recent years, they have learned swiftly and many consider that the Eagles will be a permanent threat to the big guns of rugby in future tournaments.

The Eagles were not the first American team to play in Hong Kong. In 1978, a bunch of happy Hawaiians came calling. Sevens were until then used as season-opening games in Hawaii to demonstrate to players and officials how unfit everyone was. After 1978, rugby in Hawaii was never to be the same again. The Hawaiians showed a carefree, sporting approach to the game, summed up by their garlands and floral shorts. The crowd liked them and they loved Hong Kong and they went home to preach the Sevens gospel. They did this with such effect that the Island's seven-a-side tournament swiftly turned into the premier rugby event on the Hawaiian calendar. Hawaii came twice to Hong Kong and because it remains unaffiliated to the Mainland USA Union hopes for more invitations in the future. But even if they never come back as a team, says Hawaii RF Union president, Ati So'o, the spirit of the Hong Kong Sevens continues to thrive in the islands and works its magic on the playing fields at Diamond Head.

WALES:

Coalmines, chapel, choir, and rugby. Without one of these four cultural and historical props, Wales would not be Wales. Especially without rugby. The sound of "Land of Our Fathers" rising in melodic lilt over Cardiff Arms Park is ingrained deep into Welsh life and the players from pithead and port have taken their national colours and pride to every part of the civilised [rugby playing] world. Like the other three home unions of Britain, Wales has never sent a national side to the Sevens. But the Hong Kong Welsh, strong of voice in the stands as well as actively evident on the field, have had the chance to cheer the next best thing to a national team in the form of Crawshay's Welsh. This unique organisation of wandering rugby enthusiasts makes regular forays outside the gentle hills and valleys of their homeland, not only to other parts of Britain but to Europe. In 1984, when they came to Hong Kong, they had never ventured far from home. The sight of huge leeks waving from the stands and the sound of the gentle, soaring music of the valleys from the assembled Welsh choir in the stands made them feel at home.

Most Welshmen feel at home anywhere near a rugby ball. In no part of Britain has the game held such a tight grasp on the general public as in Wales. For generations, men have gone straight from work to strenuous play, from pit to pitch, from the coal face to the goal line to follow the native inclination to pick up a ball and run with it.

Since 1922, many of the most talented of Welsh players have been performing their wonders as part of Crawshay's Welsh. The remarkable founder of this organisation was a self-taught speaker of the Welsh language, a much-honoured military hero and a lion of the rugby field. He formed the club which still bears his name to encourage more sporting links between the players of Wales and to persuade them to play together away from the rivalries of their home clubs. The success of his idea has seen more than 250 international players take to the field over the years in the distinctive maroon jerseys of the club. As one of the premier rugby nations on earth, Wales' appearance in the Hong Kong Sevens was long overdue.

WESTERN SAMOA:

Samoa for decades was split between two colonial powers, New Zealand and the United States. When the Kiwis left and half of the chain of islands gained independence under the name of Western Samoa, they left behind them a legacy of rugby. This love for the game has taken the Samoans to fields across the Pacific to other island neighbours like Fiji, the Solomons and Tonga, to New Zealand and in junior teams to Canada. Since their first appearance in Hong Kong in 1978, the Samoans have put up lively performances. But never have they done better than in the huge upset in the Cup championship quarter final in 1983 when they gave a lesson to their own teachers — and trounced the mighty All Blacks in a 4-0 game that was the shock of the Tournament.

In 1924, Fiji toured Western Samoa and played in Apia, the capital. It was Fiji's first overseas international game and made history in more ways than one. Kick-off was at 7am so Samoan players could get to work. A large tree, said to be sacred, was growing on the centre line and players had to duck around it as well as swerve to avoid opposition tacklers. In some ways, the Samoans have always been overshadowed by Fiji and Tonga. But this hasn't stopped them trying. In 1979, Taufisi Salesa, his nation's sprint champion, was named fastest man of the Hong Kong Sevens Tournament.

1978

With four more countries invited to the Tournament, the base of the contest pyramid was broadened. It meant 38 games instead of 22 and in turn this meant the competition had to spread over an entire weekend. "Two days of non-stop rugby," the sportwriters forecast with glee. Indeed, things had got so complicated that data on the teams was fed into a computer which provided the draw for pool matches. The Chief Justice, Sir Denys Roberts, read out the computer's verdict at the now-traditional draw at the Hong Kong Hilton. The computer, all agreed as they studied the draw, had by and large done a very fair job. The Big Four — Australia, Japan, New Zealand and Fiji — each headed a different pool. The titans would not clash immediately. Tension would build up through the elimination rounds on April 15, the experts proclaimed, and excitement would reach unbearable levels on the Sunday. True, but that was not all the story because the thrills started seconds after Fiji put their foot to the ball to begin the first game of the '78 Sevens. The computer had matched them against unfortunate newcomers Bahrain.

Airborne without wings, this ambitious Hawaiian soars up and away towards the try line.

Bahrain's players were more accustomed to playing on sand. But they swiftly adapted their tactics to the mud of the Football Club and proved a popular and speedy side.

In keeping with the original aims, the four additions to the list of countries were from the Asia-Pacific regions. From the Gulf, Bahrain sent a team of expatriates, experienced Sevens men who had plenty of practice against teams from other sheikdoms. Papua New Guinea was represented for the first time and the early speculation was that they could pose a major threat. Hawaii put the Stars and Stripes into consideration and from the vastness of the Pacific came yet another team of high-spirited islanders, the Samoans.

Previous page: Manawatu proved too speedy for the opposition in 1978 and the Flying Farmers from New Zealand marked up some runaway victories like this win over Japan.

By now, a pattern had developed which was to continue year after year. As soon as the date for the next Sevens was announced, pressmen around the region started swapping notes on teams and players. This meant that Hong Kong spectators were remarkably well informed about the visitors. This year, they read, Thailand was sending a strong team in which veterans had been mixed with fleet newcomers. The Sri Lankan selectors had stuck to the old familiar faces who had carried the ball so pluckily over recent years. The Tongans arrived first at Kai Tak Airport and as they disembarked said they had been practising for months. There was much muttering about the Hawaiians; they had defeated the strong Wellington provincial side a few months earlier in New Zealand. The limelight of pre-games speculation, however, was reserved for the big names from the big nations. The Kiwis were back, of course, and seemed pretty certain of things. Once again, they had not sent a national team and were represented by the provincial team of Manawatu. But the men from the quiet farming valley posed a major threat because they were New Zealand's national Sevens and Fifteens champions. Press reports from Wellington said the Kiwi farmers were coming with every intention of going back home with the championship cup to add to the Ranfurly Shield, New Zealand's premier rugby prize, and other trophies in the Manawatu clubhouse. There was much reflection, too, on the Australians. And the Japanese this year had managed to send a full squad of internationals. It was obvious they meant business. As for Hong Kong, the selectors were watching carefully every game played in the Colony. They were looking for players with flair and imagination, men with a turn of speed and dazzling footwork, runners with brains to outwit the wily Fijians, strength to battle through the Kiwi line and pace to outstrip the Aussies. It was a tall order. But from the healthy Hong Kong clubs, the men who had to make the difficult choice found a variety of players that gave the necessary mix of experienced skill and youthful vigour.

As it turned out, the selectors might have done better in their hunt for a winning side to have turned their attention to Repulse Bay beach rather than the rugby grounds of Hong Kong. For weeks before the April kick-off, the skies over Hong Kong were a sullen gray. It rained every day. The ground was sodden. Cathay's jets delivering the teams swooped down over Kowloon out of an impenetrable layer of cloud that seemingly had no end. Adept as they may be at managing a rugby fixture, there was little the Hong Kong Rugby Football Union could do to order the heavens to clear. Tokkie Smith stood in the middle of the Football Club ground and looked at the sky hoping to see a glimmer of blue. He got soaked. Tokkie Smith cast his eyes upwards and couldn't see the clouds for the downpour. It rained and it rained and it rained. When the Fijians splashed out for the first game at 4.30pm, the floodlights were already on and

not having much success at penetrating the torrent. The happy Islanders were, literally, in their element; the conditions were heaven-made for their shoeless style of play. The Bahrainis, more accustomed to sand than waterlogged grounds, didn't stand a chance, although they put up a brave albeit forlorn battle. And still it rained; during one 24 hour period of the weekend, no less than three inches of rain was measured at the Royal Observatory and those huddling on the open stands swore that the downpour was concentrated directly above the stadium.

But even constant rain could not wipe the gleam of glamour off what was a magnificent weekend to remember. The newcomers brought to the stadium some delightful touches, Bahrain with their head-dresses and Hawaii with their leis of flowers and hibiscus shorts. But there was more than just show business from the new boys. They had plenty of hard, driving rugby to deliver to the crowd. Astonishingly, surprising even themselves, Bahrain defeated Singapore to take

Hongkong and Western Samoa grapple for the ball during one of the thrilling early clashes. The friendly informality of the Sevens in the old Football Club venue was a mark of its success.

The floral shorts of the colourful Hawaiians make a vivid pattern against the mud and grass of the playing field. The happy Hawaiians were popular players with the Hong Kong fans, even when they clashed enthusiastically with the home side as in this 1978 contest.

the Plate. In another upset, Papua New Guinea beat Japan. Western Samoa, too, did well, scramblng through the mud to hold the mighty Fijians down to a respectable level.

By the time semi-finals began the ground was a quagmire. The churned earth and trampled grass could not be seen beneath the lake-like surface, pitted by incessant rain, but every step a player took dragged his boots into the sludge, every tackle caused a splash like a tree falling into a flooded river. For those who sat through the downpour, the rugby was worth it. The clash between the cousins of the Tasman Sea was a memorable event with the big Aussies and Kiwis crashing head on for possession and wading through the water cutting down the racing speed of the backs. They looked, said one sodden observer, like dinosaurs grappling in the primaeval ooze. The conditions called for new tactics, and Kiwi prop Ken Maharey tried one out; instead of wading for the line, he dove for it and aquaplaned 15 metres through mud and slush. It scored a try, but put him out of the competition with injuries. He was missed in the championship

when Manawatu faced the dynamic darlings of the crowd. There was no mistaking who the stands fancied and as the giant Fijians danced and leapt onto the sodden field, they were once again greeted with a cheer. Still looking as though they were reeling from the clash with the Australians, their opponents battled on. It was a thrilling, spiralling game that had the crowds forgetting their umbrellas and standing, shouting themselves hoarse, in the rain. Slipping, sliding, splashing, the Fijians light-heartedly tossed the ball through the drenching rain as though they were on an outing at the beach. It was glorious play, magnificent rugby. Although the final score was 14-10 and Fiji had won the match by only one try, nobody was in any doubt that they were true champions. In every sense. The Kiwis cheerfully conceded them the crown.

"Those fascinating Fijians," wrote the SCM Post's Jack Beattie before the Tournament, tipping them as the winners. "The magnificent Seven," he described them when he saw his prediction come true. Magnificent was right. Everyone who saw them agreed.

Competitions — 1978

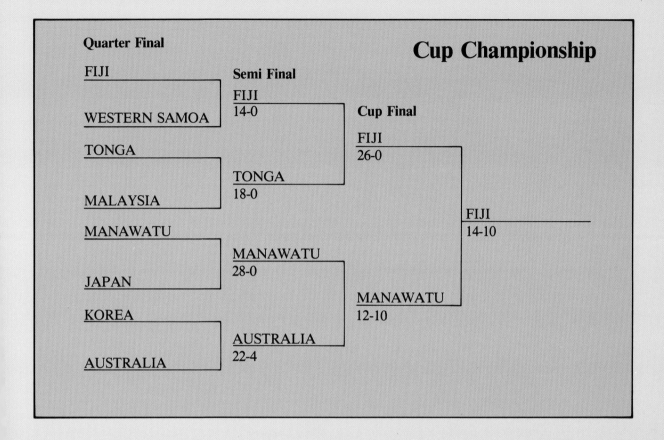

Cup Championship

Quarter Final

FIJI

WESTERN SAMOA

TONGA

MALAYSIA

MANAWATU

JAPAN

KOREA

AUSTRALIA

Semi Final

FIJI
14-0

TONGA
18-0

MANAWATU
28-0

AUSTRALIA
22-4

Cup Final

FIJI
26-0

MANAWATU
12-10

FIJI
14-10

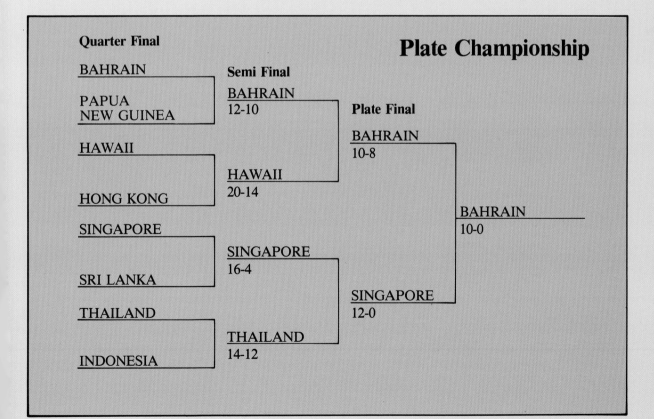

Plate Championship

Quarter Final

BAHRAIN

PAPUA
NEW GUINEA

HAWAII

HONG KONG

SINGAPORE

SRI LANKA

THAILAND

INDONESIA

Semi Final

BAHRAIN
12-10

HAWAII
20-14

SINGAPORE
16-4

THAILAND
14-12

Plate Final

BAHRAIN
10-8

SINGAPORE
12-0

BAHRAIN
10-0

Players — 1978

Australia
Andrew Slack
Paul McLean
Philip Carter
Gary Pearse
Mark Loane
Ken Wright
Greg Cornelsen
Tony Shaw
Stephen Streeter
John Howard (M)

Bahrain
Richard Turnbull
Grant Haskell
Phil Griffiths
Richard Duck
John Fidler
Ross Aldridge
Fred Simmons
Jeff Evans
Dave Billington
Bill Tyler (M)

Fiji
Pio Tiroisuva
Isimeli Batibasaga
Robert Howard
Qele Ratu
Rupeni Ravonu
Vuata Naresia
Senitiki Nasave
Kata Ratumuri

Hawaii
Gary Dill
Doug Straehley
Siope Motuapuaka
Doug Lynch
Mark Olson
Fale Tiueti
Wayne Young
Ilimi Kurusiga
Mark Kallenberger
Dr. Jack Keenan (M)

Hong Kong
Ian Parker
Drew Lamont
Jeff Bond
Paul Ogolter
John Hardie
Bryn Jones
Ian Duncan
Dave Cocks
Alistair Gumley
Peter Duncan (M)

Indonesia
Stuart Murray
Ian Kent
Peter Maiden
Ian Moakes
Mike Worrall
John Cordony
Paul Bailey
David Read
Patrick O'Flynn

Japan
Ichiro Kobayashi
Kyoichi Toyoyama
Masaru Fujiwara
Hiroshima Yamashita
Masao Yoshida
Manabu Sasada
Naoshi Kumagai
Shigetaka Mori
Hirotaka Ujino
Hisash Yokoi (M)

Korea
Min Jun-Kee
Yun Jung-Sack
Kim Yong-Hoon
An Young-Moon
Song le-Hun
Lee Jac-Moon
Lee Bong-Sun
Heo Chang-Moo
Park Kyung-Cho
Shon Du-Ohk (M)

Malaysia
Cheong Kai Yong
Ng Tat Tay
Zaharuddin bin Alias
Norman Manan
Nawawi Hassan
Jagjit Singh Bhatt
Zulkiply Abdul Aziz
Lim Say Tee
Zainuddin bin Modhammad

Manawatu (New Zealand)
Paul Broederlow
Ken Granger
Doug Rollerson
Denis Clare
Peter Cook
Ken Maharey
Grant Bowater
Terry Clare
Hugh Blair
Merlin Shannon (M)

Papua New Guinea
James Gondo
Norrane Bomai
Joe Toliman
George Mero
Thomas Kubu
Sab Doiwa
Kozap Binong
Philip Num
John Garap (M)

Singapore
Natahar Bava
Peter Brookes
Duncan Richardson
Hemi Williams
Hamzah Bin Mohamad
Teo Han Chua
Brent Cook
Mike Richardson
Bruce Mataki
Andrew Chin
Kwok Kheun Choong
Richard Vanderput

Sri Lanka
Lanil Tennekoon
Ronald Rodrigo
Frank Hubert
Michael Jayasekera
Angelo Wickremaratne
Mohan Balasuriya
Jayaprakash Rudra
Jeffrey De Jong
Gamini Fernando (M)

Thailand
Chaivat Kachasut
Tawee Klomkeaw
Van Lenburi
Somkiart Plumanas
Vate Lenburi
Ruj Sankosik
Chatupol Punsoni
Charakit Santikasem
Smitti Mukdasanit
Charuay Polprasert
Colonel Prasert Ratakarn (M)

Tonga
Pasuka Mapakaitolo
Viliami Tu'ipulotu
Valita Ma'ake
Mosese Tuipulotu
Polutele Tu'ihalamaka
Kuli Lomu
'Ikani Palu
Viliami Lutua
Samiu Hala'unga (M)

Western Samoa
Details not available

Traditions

In the first years of its lively existence, the Hong Kong Sevens swiftly established unique patterns. The gathering soon began to foster its own brand of festival behaviour, a good-hearted, openly-exhuberant, jovial friendliness, a picnic smorgasbord in which copious amounts of beer, huge hampers of food, scurrying crowds of children and roaring approval of good rugby mixed into a lively mardi gras cocktail of fun.

One of these traditions was born on that first day of play back in 1976, an incident that grew out of unhappy circumstances but which over the years developed into an integral part of Sevens lore. During the tussle in the vital semi finals of that first day's play, a violent clash flared between Fiji, the darlings of the crowd who had won the hearts of all with their flowing, flamboyant style, and the Australians. It was one of those flashpoints that come in all sports where the desire to win leads to flying fists and boots. Although the ref [quite rightly in the viewpoint of knowledgeable spectators] blamed the Fijians and sent off one of the players, the crowd sided with the underdogs and booed the Aussies. An irrational act because the players in the green-and-gold had nothing to do with the decision.

Previous page: No, he is not praying to the ball, just trying to raise himself after being forced into touch close to the goal line.

But they bore the brunt of disapproval. Despite the boos, they went on to win. But the incident was to lead to one of the most lasting signs of the Sevens and every year when the Australians run onto the field they are greeted with good-natured catcrys. "C'mon the convicts," is a familiar call. The Aussies take it with a grin; it certainly does not seem to have hampered their performances over the years because they have battled their way into most finals and won outright four years. Sometimes, more often than not, the venerable cry to the alleged ball-and-chain Down Under ancestry comes with a very distinctive and proud Aussie twang.

Traditions? They build up remarkably fast in the pressure-cooker atmosphere of the Sevens' weekends. Possibly, this is because so much is packed into so short a time. There's more rugby played, more people met, more players from more countries rubbing shoulders with more

supporters from more clubs of more races of more backgrounds than at any other half-dozen rugby gatherings. It's the rugby gathering of the clans. And that's no joke, either. When Caledonia fields a team, the long, low roar "Scot-land" echoes, proving — if any proof be necessary — the long and proud links between North Britain and her far Colony of Hong Kong, founded so long ago by sons of Scotland and still today with such a Scots heritage. Just look at the Pipe Band of the Royal Hong Kong Police, tartans flying, playing during the March Past of teams.

Tradition? The Arabic headdress of the Gulf teams and their waving banners and the cries urging on their players. The now-customary exchanges of jerseys between players who have won the respect of opponents.

Traditions? What of the clashes between the Fijians and Tongans and other Melanesians who go through their victory dances and Men of Harlech as they wave the huge plastic leeks? And the lively, lovable Solomon Islanders sending the ball spinning as high as the top of the grandstands as they run onto the ground?

It's astonishing that in such a short period such a heritage has been built up. Nowhere is this more so than on the stands where the spectators

have themselves created their own traditions. Year after year, parties of friends seem to head for the same spaces on the concrete benches, wisely bringing something warm, light and padded on which to sit. Hong Kong may not be a large place in a geographical sense, but hard-driving business that tends to take many rugby followers on endless rounds of regional travel means that the Sevens is not only a chance to watch spectacular rugby, it is an annual opportunity to see those who you haven't seen since.... well, since the last Sevens.

Far left: Young Hong Kong fans, ardent followers of the game, get the chance to have their programmes autographed by the international greats of the game. There are more signatures to be gained on the sidelines at Sookunpoo every year than anywhere else in the world.

Left: Generous help comes from the British garrison in Hong Kong. Playing fields at Stanley Fort are used for training exercises and when there is a regiment with a band stationed in Hong Kong, there is martial music at the ground. Here, the Queen's Own Highlanders gather the rugby clans for the march past.

Right: The home team always gets a big hand from the crowd. But it is likely to be mixed with jeers if the boys in blue have play in the opinion of the experts in the stands.

Bottom: Where else, visitors ask, can you see a Chinese pipe band lead the march past of teams from 24 nations in the middle of an international rugby festival? Nowhere. That's just one reason the Sevens are unique.

Next page: No, it's not the Fijians looking to the heavens for inspiration or help. The happy islanders are merely going through warm-up exercises before taking to the field.

1979

It was a season of surprises. The competitions for both Plate and Cup were to be seized exultantly by teams which had never won before. There were to be upsets aplenty on the field and the see-saw swings on the wheel of fortune kept the crowds on their feet. The players jetted in to take part in an event that was by this time, in the maturity of its fourth year, a major signpost on the international sporting map. "It is the largest sports event of its kind in the world," noted the Governor of Hong Kong, Sir Murray MacLehose, in his welcoming message to players, officials and fans. He was not the only one to heap praise on the Sevens. Rugby Unions around the world were asking how tiny Hong Kong did it. And local fans, undeterred by the wash-out the previous year, were showing their interest weeks before the competition in the most significant manner; advance ticket sales were running at record levels, noted the new Hong Kong Rugby Football Union chairman, Denis Evans, with delight.

As usual, the international rugby rumour mill was working overtime. Hong Kong businessmen on their endless sorties abroad returned with gossip and newspaper clippings about what sort of teams Hong Kong could expect to see. Tonga could not come and the full complement of 16

teams was made up by a new colour appearing on the familiar Football Club field, the jersey of Brunei. They were very much an unknown quantity and from the scanty reports Hong Kong fans read, seemed to be dominated by British expatriate players with a sprinkling of Bruneians. What was known, however, was the strength of the major teams. The awesome Aussies, it was said, had prepared a super-team. Said manager Sir Nick Shehadie: "I think this could be our year." The Kiwis were itching for another crack at the championship and had dispatched another Manawatu provincial side, a team billed as powerful and unstoppable, a steamroller of a team which would roll over the opposition. Fiji was back with their customary confidence and their winning smiles. "We wouldn't be here if we didn't think we could win," joked coach Pio Bosco Tikoisuva.

Australian manager Sir Nick Shehadie is almost as mud-splattered as the Wallaby players as they gather on the sidelines after the 1979 final. It was beer all round as the team gave an Aussie salute.

Previous page: Papua on the attack against Hawaii in the muddy Plate Championship final of 1979.

Classic rugby. A back is horizontal above the field as the ball shoots from his hands like a cannonball. In Sevens, as in the XVs format, some things never change, and a perfect pass remains forever a thing of beauty.

Hurdling a downed opponent is one way to get ahead as this players illustrates as he scrambles upfield during one of the early '79 games.

The Aussies had reason for confidence. They had never won the championship, but had always gone close. They kicked off the first ball ever 'way back in 1976, were the only team to have beaten Fiji [in a semi-final in 1976] and in 1978 had knocked up a staggering score of 116 points in three preliminary games without having a single point scored against them. They were not in Hong Kong to mess about. The Spring rains again made life miserable for the packed spectators. The Football Club was sodden again. Throughout the weekend the rain dripped dismally down but the electricity on the field made up for the lack of sunshine.

Surprise! Western Samoa downed powerful Japan. Then another surprise when Indonesia did the same. Surprise! And delight for the hometown fans when Hong Kong beat first Sri Lanka and then Thailand to romp for the first time into the championship round on the second day. Surprise! Fiji got into the final championship round as expected, but somehow some of the flair, the fire, the sparkle of previous years seemed to be missing. Surprise! Hawaii knocked Bahrain, winners of the Plate the previous year, out of the competition. And then came the shock to end them all when Korea, the tough, never-

Hong Kong on the attack and the home team, with a rare grasp of the ball, burst away from the Wallabies pack and with the roar of the crowd in their ears run the ball.

say-die underdogs, made an astonishing, determined, gritty battle to down the Fijians in the quarter finals, leaving the crowd breathless and hoarse and making the stocky Koreans favourites with the fans. This was the last fling, however, for the team from the Land of the Morning Calm. They lost the next round to the lively lads from Western Samoa who had seemingly dashed from nowhere to be suddenly in the finals. Fiji had already dispatched Hong Kong from the reckoning before their own turn came to be humbled by Korea.

But before the championship final came the game that for many was the match of the day. Ranged against each other were the giants of the Pacific, Australia and New Zealand, and both squads were determined to win. It was a game worth waiting for. Two days sitting on hard concrete in the rain was a modest price to pay to see this spectacle. The Aussies were dazzling. They had started the Tournament well and just kept getting better. They took the game to the Manawatu side, scored quickly and then did it again. The New Zealand team were simply outplayed. As were the Samoans when they trotted onto the field for a final which saw them pitted against one of the most stylish, skillful and successful teams ever to play in the Hong Kong Sevens. The Wallabies were magic. The giant forwards got plenty of ball and gave it to the speedy backs who romped home with it. Time after time. The score was a crushing 39-3 defeat for Western Samoa and the result faithfully reflected the play. It had taken Australia four years to snatch the championship, but as the players staggered exhausted, muddy and wet from the field, the cheering crowds could tell from their jaunty grins that the effort had been worthwhile.

It is not often that sporting news and views makes the editorial columns of newspapers. But the 1979 Sevens did it. The SCM Post commented: "More than anything else, it is the game that scores. Normally, rugby has a limited following in Hong Kong outside the international matches. But the seven-a-side variety opens up the play, shortens the duration of each match and makes for a fast, robust and exciting game. On top of this, when most of the best teams from the Asian-Pacific rim come to compete the competition assumes the form of a rugby olympiad. Game follows game in swift succession; little wonder that the stadium fills up almost from the first whistle and holds the crowd until the last. Each year, moreover, the competition improves. And while the giants, like Australia, New Zealand and Fiji dominate the play, their monopoly is being increasingly challenged by teams such as Korea, Western Samoa, Tonga, Japan and New Guinea."

There could be a trophy for the most popular team, the paper suggested. If there was, it said, the 1979 winners would have been Korea for their giant-killing win over the Fijians.

Begrimed and battered after two days' hard play, the victorious Australians and their equally-exhausted coach, Sir Nicholas Shehadie raise cans of "Aussie champagne" to mark their victory in the traditional manner.

Competitions — 1979

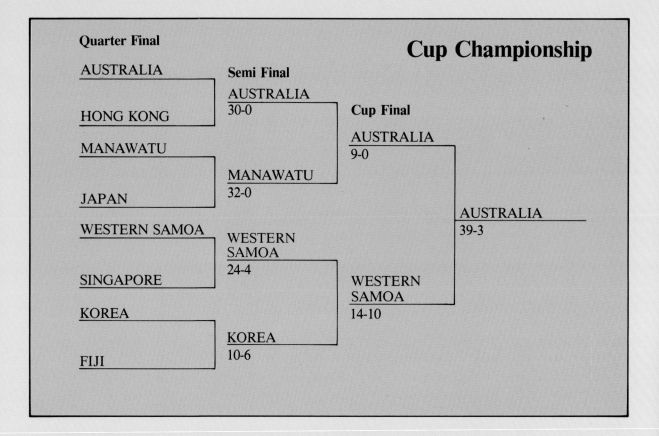

Cup Championship

Quarter Final

AUSTRALIA

HONG KONG

MANAWATU

JAPAN

WESTERN SAMOA

SINGAPORE

KOREA

FIJI

Semi Final

AUSTRALIA
30-0

MANAWATU
32-0

WESTERN SAMOA
24-4

KOREA
10-6

Cup Final

AUSTRALIA
9-0

WESTERN SAMOA
14-10

AUSTRALIA
39-3

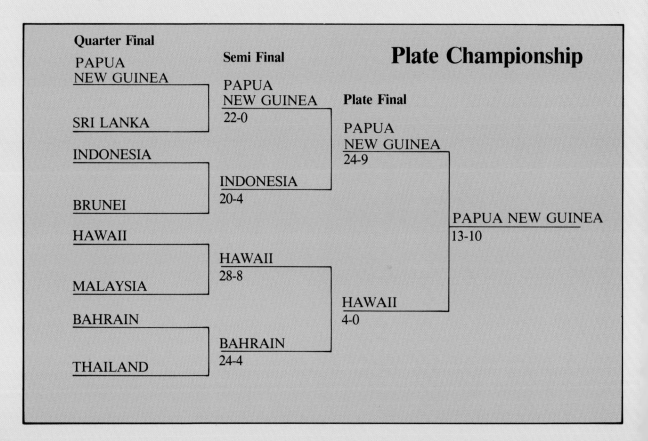

Plate Championship

Quarter Final

PAPUA NEW GUINEA

SRI LANKA

INDONESIA

BRUNEI

HAWAII

MALAYSIA

BAHRAIN

THAILAND

Semi Final

PAPUA NEW GUINEA
22-0

INDONESIA
20-4

HAWAII
28-8

BAHRAIN
24-4

Plate Final

PAPUA NEW GUINEA
24-9

HAWAII
4-0

PAPUA NEW GUINEA
13-10

Players — 1979

Australia
Roger Gould
Tom Barker
Andy Stewart
Steve Rowley
Peter McLean
Glen Ella
Mark Ella
Geoff Richards
John Maxwell
Sir Nicholas Shehadie (M)

Bahrain
Brent Humphries
Chris Hook
Colin Gregory
Phil Wade
Michael Stapleton
David Billington
George Duffy
Richard Duck
Grant Haskell
Bill Tyler (M)

Brunei
Peter Greaves
Cliff Berry
Malcolm Braithwaite
Daven Chiuh
Stephen Hayes
Pat Wilson
Peter Smith
John Wright
Mohd Roger

Fiji
Ilami Lutumailagi
Vuata Naresia
Sela Gutugutuwai
Senitiki Nasave
Josefa Rauto
Tanielo Driu Ralumu
Robert Howard
Isimeli Batibasaga
Qele Ratu
Pio Bosco Tikoisuva (M)

Hawaii
Doug Straehley
Doug Lynch
Gary Dill
Wayne Young
Matelan Sekona
Tau Sevelo
Valeti Langi
Ula Lomu
Ali Mokofisi
Mark Olson
Jack Keenan (M)

Hong Kong
Bryn Jones
Chris Wynne-Potts
Graeme Blackwood
Peter Duncan
Bernie Byrne
Harry Bingley
Colin Heck
Brian Clesham
Ian Duncan
Gus Cunningham (M)

Indonesia
Rob Church
J. Leighton
C. Strudwick
Pat O'Flynn
C. Wokes
I. Hughes
Peter Maiden
Ian Kent
Stuart Murray
Stephen Hayes

Japan
Masao Yoshida
Kyoichi Toyoyama
Shigetaka Mori
Ichiro Kobayashi
Naoshi Kumagai
Hiroshi Yamashita
Manabu Sasada
Masaru Fujiwara
Hirotaka Ujino

Korea
Lee Jae-Moon
Lee Bong-Sun
Jung Hea-Keuk
Kim Yong-Hoon
Park No-Je
An Kwang-Seung
Han Moon-Man
You Jea Soo
Kim Kyung-Bea (M)

Malaysia
Zulkiply Aziz
Zaharuddin Alias
Lim Say Tee
Ibrahim Osman
Zainuddin Mohammad
Mohammad Yat
Rahim Yusoff Ronnie Yeoh
Mubin Jerman
Boon Hoon Chee
Loke Kai Heng (M)

Manawatu (New Zealand)
Hugh Blair
Allan Innes
Ken Granger
Ken Maharey
John Gilmer
Terry Clare
Dennis Clare
Mac Thompson
Graham Hamer

Papua New Guinea
Kozap Binong
Sab Doiwa
Norrane Bomai
Valeti Langi
Matelav Sekona
Ali Mokofisi
Ula Lomu
Tau Sevelo
John Garap (M)

Singapore
Song Koon Poh
Jarmal Singh
Hamzah Mohd
Bohari Sarmani
Frank Kwok
Ong Poh Wah
Chooi Kam Kong
Andrew Chin
David Quek
Buzari Kavat
Natahar Bava (M)

Sri Lanka
Jeffrey De Jong
Lanil Tennekoon
Jeffrey Yu
Bharatha Hegoda
Michael Jayaskekera
Mohan Balasuriya
Hafi Abdeen
Chandrishan Perera
S. Navaratnam (M)

Thailand
Van Lenburi
Vate Lenburi
Chankit Santikasem
Chaivat Kachasut
Boonlert Kanchanachongkol
Songtham Allapachana
Suvit Mapaisansin
Supparat Allapachana
Pitaya Thepbanterng

Western Samoa
Taufisi Salesa
Feausiga Sililoto
Arona Palamo
Simanu Simi
Andrew Leavasa
Kenape Tu-u-au
Derek Saifoloi
Tufua Lafaaili
Tomanu Heather

In the stands, there are no managers on hand to see the spectators do not drink. The festival is a fun, family time, and like other mardi gras and happy gatherings a big part of it is involved in eating, drinking and being merry. The beer girls who keep the stands afloat in a sea of amber fluid are probably unaware they are keeping alive an ancient and honoured rugby tradition.

Great Unseen

When 20,000 spectators cheer as two teams run onto the grass at Sookunpoo, much of the applause should go to an army of men and women who are never seen. They are the unknown, unsung workers without whom the Cathay Pacific-Hongkong Bank Invitation Sevens could never take place. There are the Sponsors, of course. And the officials of the Hong Kong Rugby Football Union, men who by the time the first kick-off comes around are footworn and weary after months of administrative chores. But there are many, many more. You could call them The Great Unseen.

For weeks before the Tournament starts, all year round, in fact, groundsmen and workers have been trying to prepare the pitch. Every tuft of grass has been cared for. If it has been a long, dry winter, hoses have been on to try to bring a bit of green to the grass. If the rains have come early, what mopping-up can be done has been attempted. There are voluntary doctors ready to treat the wounded on the field and those who have become too tired and emotional on the stands. Non-stop excitement can prove too much for some spectators and the doctors are called on

Previous page: After the mini-rugby boys get too old to play curtain raising matches, they graduate to become ball boys. It is a position greatly sought after, giving them a worm's eye view of the play.

to treat them, too. St. Johns Ambulance volunteers in their smart uniforms are based around the ground ready to run stretchers and emergency first aid kits onto the field. On the sidelines, touch judges run miles back and forth with the play to flag for the referee the exact spot where a ball has gone into touch. Ball boys from local clubs are on the spot to throw in a fresh ball so play can continue promptly.

On the stands, a corps of caterers dispense food and drink to the thousands for whom watching the Sevens is thirsty work, indeed. The beer-selling girls weaving through the good-

natured crowd with jugs of beer and jaunty smiles have become a feature of the weekend. After a couple of jugs, some customers cheer the girls in the stands as enthusiastically as the players on the field. Caring for 20,000 people for two days is akin to being city government of a fair-sized community. You need all the basic infrastructure that a town requires. Communications within the sizeable city that exists in the ground comes through a loudspeaking system, the voice of Pat MacLachlan that carries messages on such community topics as missing children, abandoned cars, calls for senior government officials to call their offices — urgently! — and items of information on upcoming games. For this system, electricians are needed. And, of course, there are policemen called for to ensure smooth running of the traffic flow outside. The Royal Hong Kong Police

carries out this duty, one of their myriad of tasks in keeping the territory safe.

The police are also on hand in a very different role. Traditionally, it is the Police Pipe Band that plays in the centre of the field during the March Past in the afternoon of the Sunday. "A Chinese pipe band!" Some of the visitors are enthralled. But it is, after all, Hong Kong, and the Highlands of Scotland have historically provided many of the men in the police. What could be more natural in Hong Kong, and more appropriate for an international sporting event in Asia, than a Chinese pipe band?

Opposite page top: Boosting the presence of the Union's own security patrols, private security staff are on duty to help maintain order. There is seldom any trouble with the fun-loving crowd, missing children are the biggest headache and announcers often give plaintive pleas over the broadcasting system when lost youngsters with big appetites eat them out of ice-cream.

Opposite page bottom: On hand, but thankfully seldom needed, are the ladies of the St. John's Ambulance Brigade. Every year, the Brigade dispatches a solid core of volunteers to the ground. They are on hand to bring expert assistance to players and fans who come to grief, a source of insurance against injury.

Left: In the grandstand at the end of the ground, players wait anxiously for their next match. Behind the scenes, Jean Astin does a great job keeping the tea, coffee and orange juice flowing. Countless gallons of hot drinks keep players happy.

Below: Watching the Sevens for a 10-hour stretch gives a hearty appetite and stands are located throughout the stadium to make sure nobody goes hungry and to sell souvenirs as in this photograph.

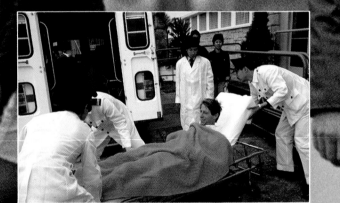

Medical assistance is always as close as the sidelines during the games. Rugby is a contest of skill and strength and minor injuries are accepted as part of the game. But medics with specialist skills in sporting injuries are stationed at the ground to give instant aid. These remedial gymnasts will massage out twisted tendons.

Insert left: Ambulance services are seldom needed. But they are on hand if injury occurs.

Insert right: These has never been a major injury during the Sevens. One reason is because volunteer doctors, nurses, paramedics and experts in sports injuries are always on hand to administer prompt aid.

1980

CATHAY PACIFIC HONGKONG BANK

7

1980
CATHAY PACIFIC
HONGKONG BANK

**INTERNATIONAL
SEVEN-A-SIDE
RUGBY
CHAMPIONSHIP**

12TH - 13TH APRIL 1980
HONG KONG FOOTBALL CLUB
STADIUM

ORGANISED BY:
THE HONG KONG RUGBY
FOOTBALL UNION

HK$5.00

April is a fickle month in Hong Kong. The seasons are changing. The winter monsoon is dying, but can bring forth some last, stubborn surges of bitterly cold air bursting gustily, down from frigid Gobi desert and icy Siberian steppes. The month can also smile and produce brilliant, humid days with bright sunshine. Or it can bring sullen overcast skies with endless drizzles. Or it can herald the rainy season a month before schedule and produce downpours which swamp the coastal fringe of South China. In 1980, the changeable season brought solid, steady rain. Then more drenching rains. And just as everyone looked at the heavens and thought, surely, there could not be any more water up there, the skies truly opened and a cloudburst dumped oceans of water on the sodden pitch. Nobody was quite sure what the grass was like; it was under a foot of water. The weathermen held out little hope of improvement. But as an unseen sun tried with no success to pierce the murk above Happy Valley on Saturday, April 12, there was only one thing certain; lots of people would be playing rugby there later that day.

The groundsmen inspect the pitch!

To celebrate the first five years, competition organisers in 1980 cast ever wider their nets to bring in two more top teams from abroad. Included in the 15 groups of players swarming exhuberantly off Cathay jets were a national team from Canada and the Co-Optimists from Scotland. The North Americans were giants, men like Ro Hindson of British Columbia who reared almost two metres tall and weighed well over 100 kilos. He looked, one spectator remarked, like the Rocky Mountains on legs. The Canadians were very much an unknown quantity on the international rugby scene. And they arrived in Hong Kong determined to let the rest of the world

Opposite page: Like gladiators in a muddy arena, weary Manawatu and Australian players take a welcome break from play.

know they had been playing rugby — come rain, hail, snow or blizzard — for 115 years. The Co-Optimists arrived from the homeland of the Sevens. They had every intention of taking the championship cup home with them when they returned to Scotland. Dubai replaced Bahrain as representatives from the Middle East. Japan's top referee, Hirochi Nonomura, came to officiate at the competition, adding even more to the international flavour. The presence of new teams from far places was proof both of the importance of the championships and Hong Kong's growing role as a centre for international sport, said the chairman of the new sponsors, Michael Sandberg of the Hongkong and Shanghai Banking Corporation. Six months before the kick-off, the corporate headquarters of Rothmans, the tobacco company which from the start had been an ardent supporter and co-sponsor of the Tournament, announced it was carrying out an overall survey of the role it played in sporting events. Reluctantly, the firm announced it was withdrawing from active participation in the Sevens. It was sad for the Union organisers to say farewell to staunch friends that the local representatives of the company had become over the years, but a swift decision by The Bank, Hong Kong's largest financial institution, guaranteed continuity.

That well-known virus, Sevens Fever, was by 1980 definitely catching. For weeks, the usual speculation had been bandied around the taprooms and clubhouses. The Co-optimists were the ones to watch, was the verdict. "The super-seven," they were dubbed. Their captain, Lions veteran Andy Irvine, admitted the Scots had no idea of what sort of opposition they would meet. Teams like Malaysia and Sri Lanka were a complete mystery to them, he said. They had never heard of Papua New Guinea players until they scrambled through a game of touch rugby in a warm-up practice session with some of the players from the Papua New Guinea side — which promptly ran away to a four-touchdown win. Dubai, other newcomers, were as unknown to the Sevens regulars as the Papuans were to the Scots. Sri Lanka came with youthful new faces in their side. Korea was fielding its trusty veterans. Japan looked its normal formidable self.

Local selectors looked carefully at the teams they were likely to come up against. As usual, the opposition appeared rugged and when the draw came out there were mixed feelings. Hong Kong was to play against Dubai and Singapore in the preliminary rounds. They won both games and went onto the field against mighty Fiji.

In full cry, the massive American Eagles forwards pound after the ball in their match with Thailand in 1980. The newcomers from North America surprised many fans from more traditional rugby strongholds with their flair, pace and skill.

Hong Kong snatched the lead with two brilliant tries and the local fans went mad with excitement as the home team battled valiantly to hold on to their unexpected lead. Finally, they went down 12-8, a very respectable showing against the South Pacific veterans.

Spectators had problems following the matches. A couple of minutes into play and all 14 players were coloured the same rich, dark brown. Occasionally, glimpses of their jerseys could be seen. That was when they had been tackled or slipped into the inches-deep water on the pitch and the impromptu swim had given them a swift dousing. There were fears that some of the mini-rugby boys playing a demonstration match could disappear and drown in 18 inches of water which covered one end of the ground. After scrums and tackles, referees and parents counted heads to see that the correct number of boys had emerged.

The conditions were atrocious. Many of the spectators out on the open stands, huddled under umbrellas, were as wet as the players. But the games went on. Firemen were called in and put their pumps into the surface water to try to drain off some of the excess. Thousands of gallons poured through the hoses into drains along Sports Road. But the rain kept coming and the levels in the ground kept rising. Despite the appalling weather and the lake-like surface of the ground, skill still told. The four seeded teams all got to the Cup semi final where Fiji put down the Australians and the Scots downed the Manawatu side. By the time the finalists plodded onto the mire for the final game, a kick-off was out of the question. The ball just floated away. There was a real danger, officials conceded, that a brand new danger could be added to the long list of rugby hazards; drowning. During the day, as the rain kept coming down and the ground conditions continued to worsen, organisers discussed cancellation. No, said the players. No said the visiting officials. No, no, never, said the crowds in the stands, soaked but exhilarated. Play on. So on they played, and those who witnessed the last match through the rain and the bow waves caused by crashing players sliding and splashing towards an invisible goal line all agreed that the dousing had been worth it. It was a game in which fortunes see-sawed. The Scots led. The Fijians grabbed the reins back again with a thrilling try after a blistering high-speed wade by Taniela Nayate Ralumu and the Islanders won yet another Sevens 12-8.

"We knew we could do it," Fijian coach Ilaitia Tuisese said as his team washed areas of mud out of their hair before the post-game celebrations. "All Fijians know how to swim."

Competitions — 1980

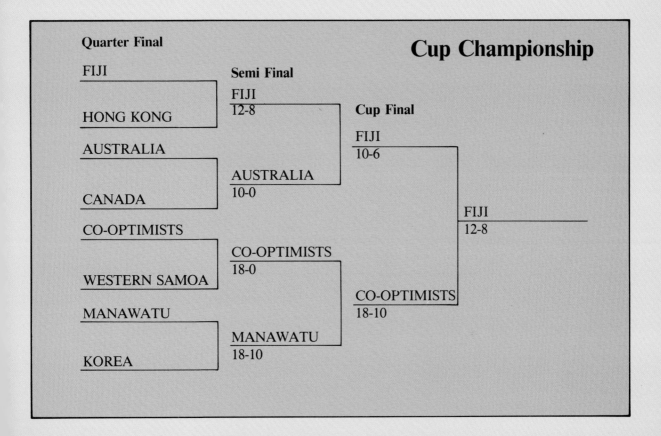

Cup Championship

Quarter Final

FIJI

HONG KONG

AUSTRALIA

CANADA

CO-OPTIMISTS

WESTERN SAMOA

MANAWATU

KOREA

Semi Final

FIJI
12-8

AUSTRALIA
10-0

CO-OPTIMISTS
18-0

MANAWATU
18-10

Cup Final

FIJI
10-6

CO-OPTIMISTS
18-10

FIJI
12-8

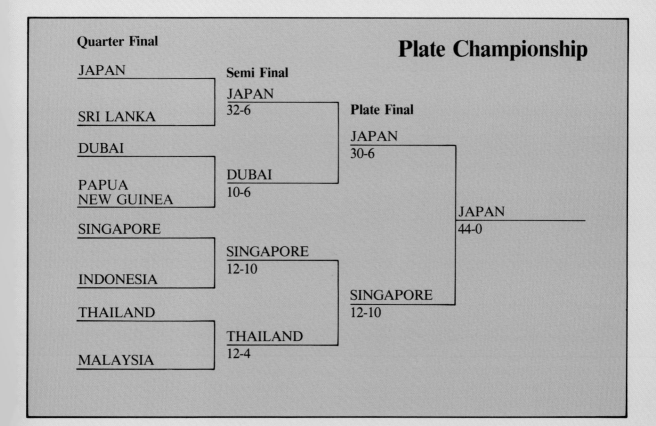

Plate Championship

Quarter Final

JAPAN

SRI LANKA

DUBAI

PAPUA
NEW GUINEA

SINGAPORE

INDONESIA

THAILAND

MALAYSIA

Semi Final

JAPAN
32-6

DUBAI
10-6

SINGAPORE
12-10

THAILAND
12-4

Plate Final

JAPAN
30-6

SINGAPORE
12-10

JAPAN
44-0

Players — 1980

Australia
Andy Stewart
Mark Ella
Glen Ella
John Maxwell
Geoff Richards
Peter McLean
Peter Carse
Michael O'Connor
Brendan Moon
Sir Nicholas Shehadie (M)

Canada
Hans de Goede
Gary Grant
Andrew Bibby
Rob Greig
Spence McTavish
Bill Monaghan
Ro Hindson
Garry Hirayama
Ray Rogers

Co-Optimists
Mike Biggar
Alex Brewster
John Rutherford
Roger Baird
Andy Irvine
Gordon Hunter
Jim Calder
David Brewster
Peter Steven
Sir John Orr (M)

Dubai
Gary Grant
David McLernon
Peter Rhodes
Patrick Fegan
Harry Millington
Michael Hooke
Maurice Nicholson
Peter Whicher
Robin Edwards

Fiji
Ilaitia Tuisese
Josefa Rauto
Ilami Lutumailagi
Paula Yaisake
Lepani Tagicakibau
Rupeni Ravonu
Sela Tugutuwai
Taniela Nayate Ramulu
Dominiko Manaseitava

Hong Kong
Ken Morrison
Brian Clesham
John Heptonstall
Mark Gritten
Jon Jenkins
Andy Hickling
Greg Knight
Brett McDonald
Ian Duncan
Gus Cunningham (M)

Indonesia
Pat O'Flynn
Dave Evans
Peter Maiden
Tim Hutton
Richard Edwards
Michael Worrall
Ian Kent
Rob Church
Dave Read

Japan
Mituru Sakamoto
Ichiro Kobayashi
Hirotaka Ujino
Yuji Matsuo
Shigetaka Mori
Mitsuyiki Fujisaki
Osamu Watahiki
Hikaru Kawaji
Hideo Tojima
Hisashi Yokoi (M)

Korea
Park Ki-Hang
Han Dong-Ho
Song le-Hoon
Youn Jun-Soek
Moon Young-Chen
Song No-II
Song Youn-Ho
Myrung Ro-Koun
You Jei-Pil
Yoon Won-Ho (M)

Malaysia
Ali Noor
Zulkiply Aziz
Rahim Yusoff
Shaari Safari
Sree Pathmanathan
Ghafar Rejab
Tan Ewe Hock
Lim Say Tee
Nik Hashim

Manawatu (New Zealand)
Stu Fleming
Mark Donalson
John Gilmer
Michael O'Callaghan
Alan Innes
Ken Maharey
Terry Clare
Lachlan Cameron
Denis Clare

Papua New Guinea
I. Pamoa
Thomas V. Kubu
Martin Bingeding
John Farapo
W. Pilisa
Sab Doiwa
Herman Wakeri
Steve Gidima

Singapore
Andrew Chin
Hamzah Mohd
Burzari Kayat
Frank Kwok
Song Koon Poh
Ong Poh Hua
Chooi Kam Kong
David Quek
Lim Khoon Huat
Natahar Bava (M)

Sri Lanka
Bharatha Hegoda
Ajith Silva
Hisham Abdeen
L. Tennakoon
Saman Jayasinghe
Angelo Wicremaratne
Rohan Hameed
Rohantha Tilak Peiris
S. Navaratnam (M)

Thailand
Supparut Allapachana
Chutchaval Thanavarchorn
Suvit Lamsam
Somsak Puekpan
Van Lenburi
Boonlert Kanchanachongkol
Somkiat Plummanus
Sataya Tepbunterng
Tanin Patamasingh

Western Samoa
Arona Palamo
Tuufua Seumanutafa
Ricky Schmidt
P. Grey
Foua Toloa
Andrew Leavasa
Taufusi Salesa
P. Schmidt
O. Natia

Referees

Ask any middle-aged man why he spends most weekends and a fair number of evenings running around a football field blowing a whistle and the answer will probably be something similar to that given by John Stonham. "I've got so much pleasure out of the game that I want to try to put a little something back into it," is the explanation given by the president of the Hong Kong Society of Rugby Football Union Referees. He has been doing this for some time; he began coaching when he was 39 and spent 16 active years adjudicating on the grass. For the past five years as president he spends more time on the sidelines watching others play and referee, but still takes out his whistle for the annual Old and Bold Game traditionally held in Hong Kong every year on January 1.

Refereeing Sevens, he contends, is in some ways easier than judging the rights and wrongs of XVs. For a start, the games are much shorter and there is less time for ill will to build up among rival sides both striving to win. Secondly, the faster format of the game, the running, passing movements, give less opportunity for hard body contact. And because there are less than half the number of men on the field than in the XVs game, any infractions are much more visible to both referees and spectators. The results speak for themselves; in the hundreds of games in the decade of the Tournament in Hong Kong, only one person has ever been sent off the field and that was in the first year. This is an incredible record and yet another testament to the spirit of the competition.

Referees are changing with the times. A couple of decades ago, they were almost invariably men in their 40s who had played all their lives and wanted to continue. But as they slowed down and got a bit heavier, their roles on the field inevitably changed and instead of carrying a ball in their hands, they carried the law book of rugby in their heads. In more recent years, younger men had been added to the referees' roll, sometimes because injuries on the rugby field have meant that it is hazardous for keen players to take a more direct part in the game. Whatever the reason for their job as refs, the men who do it at the Sevens are dedicated to a few simple ideals. They strive to keep the game moving, to see that no side gets an advantage by breaking or bending the laws, to ensure that fast, moving play continues and to eliminate as far as possible any interruption in play. The men who try to attain these difficult aims come from every walk of life. Off the field, they are teachers and engineers, policemen or insurance executives, businessmen or civil servants. On the field, they are fast-moving enforcers of the universal laws of rugby laid

Previous page: Actions speak louder than words. They need to on a field in which a New Zealand ref many find himself laying down the law in a game between Koreans and Thais. Nobody may speak each other's language, but all of them are conversant with the laws of rugby.

REFEREES ... Living up to the old adage that they are blind, referees jokingly don dark glasses and use white sticks to help them find their way past the stands in a part of the march past that has become a traditional spoof. The jeers, catcalls and boos they receive are taken in good heart.

down by the court of appeal and the parliament of rugby, the International Rugby Football Board. For the first few years of the Hong Kong Sevens the referees came from Hong Kong. Then, it was felt that the ideals and interests of the international game would be promoted in Asia if refs were invited from other lands. Since the ice-breaking Korean Woo Ho Yun came in 1979, refs from many lands have helped keep the games moving smoothly. They have come from Japan, Thailand, Australia, New Zealand, England, Scotland, Wales, Ireland and Canada. Although refereeing customs and standards may differ in various countries, the laws of rugby are universal.

Sides which win games are almost invariably pleased with the referees and touch judges. Losers are not always so philosophical. Sometimes, after the game, unhappy players will approach referees and tell them that the decisions they made were not correct. Often, the complaints are not phrased so politely, claims John Stonham and other veteran refs. After the Fiji-Scottish Borders semi-final in 1983, players politely asked senior Welsh referee Ken Parfitt if he had any more engagements on the field. Why no, said the bemused ref. Whereupon he was promptly given a mud bath in the quagmire. It was an experience he underwent with good humour.

Above: He may be blind, he may be stupid ... but he is NEVER wrong. So goes the old joke about rugby referees. It's part of the lore of the game that refs must be devoid of all senses, but players know well that the men who act as judges on the field are wise in the ways of rugby. When their whistles blow, play stops.

Insert: REFEREES..... The ref is the only person who can be readily identified in this section of a muddy battle.

Next pages: Always close to the ball, a ref is where the action is during this clash between a Korean and Australian.

Next pages insert: Between two rows of forwards, a referee stands in contemplative mood.

It was also an experience rare for a member of the august body of rugby referees. Although in the heat of fast and furious movement on the field, players may disagree with their rulings, it is a fundamental of rugby that the referee's word is the ultimate law and, no matter if it is felt to be incorrect, must be obeyed.

Every rugby referee knows the old refrain that is engraved on plaques in rugby clubs in every corner of the globe. So do most players.

It reads:
"The referee is always right.

"Stubborn perhaps, misinformed maybe, incorrect possibly, blind to innovation probably, uncompromising sometimes, and occasionally... though very infrequently... downright stupid.

"But NEVER WRONG."

1981

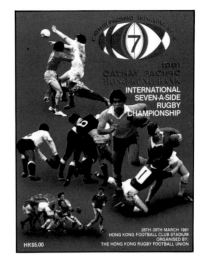

Speculation began early for the sixth year of the Sevens. Seven months before kick-off Jack Beattie was reporting in the South China Morning Post that it would be the most spectacular carnival yet, the greatest-ever rugby spectacular. There would be four more teams. All the old faces now so well known on the Football Club arena would be there. Tonga would be back. Muscat would fly a flag from the Gulf. And some exciting new sides like the British Barbarians, the American Eagles and the Argentine Pumas would be invited. Hong Kong fans did not know much about the Pumas but word soon began to circulate about a fellow called Hugo Porta, the Argentine captain, a man who had won national caps for the past decade and a player generally reckoned to be the best stand-off half in the world. Gossip was not confined to the forms of the various teams. Jack Johnston, the Union's new chairman, was just as concerned with the support the event needed from Mother Nature. The drenchings of previous years, hopefully, would be avoided. The weekend picked for the Sevens was a few weeks earlier than in the soaking history of the festival, late March instead of mid April. The Royal Observatory had been consulted and looking up

Against bigger opponents the doughty Japanese hold their line.

old records announced that this particular weekend had a blessed habit of being dry. This would be welcome news to the long-suffering fans, Beattie wrote. His editor evidently agreed with these sentiments because at the end of the 1980 Tournament the paper called for investigations to see if drainage could be improved. History, the paper noted, was against the chances of this happening because the site was once a swamp, then a paddy field before becoming a sports ground. And the surrounding hills acted like a huge natural bowl which funnelled every drop of rain that fell down to the mouth of Happy Valley, astride which rose the

Opposite page: The Pumas brought to the Sevens a dash of colour from South America where the Argentine is by far the greatest rugby playing country on the continent. The Pumas played with a speed and ferocity that lived up to their name.

Onto the field at the Football Club go the Co-Optimists on their initial visit in 1980. The immortal Andy Irvine — capped countless times for Scotland and the Lions — was a star turn at the Sevens. He is Number 15.

Football Club stadium.

Weather aside, Jack Johnston and the other Union officials had plenty about which to worry. The Tournament had been expanded once again. This year, 20 teams would parade around the stadium in the march past. With the increased pool of teams, there would be more games, no fewer than 51 matches. It would be non-stop thrills, a feast of football, the greatest rugby show on earth, the sporting press exulted.

The draw gave press, players and followers plenty to think about. Most of the seeded teams faced plenty of high hurdles before they were assured a place in the Sunday afternoon finals. With uncertainty and upsets being the name of the game, the luck of the draw pitted some unknown Davids against prominent Goliaths. There were four pools, each of five teams. Hong Kong officials lamented their luck; the home team had to face Fiji in their first game. In other pools, Goliaths faced Goliaths. The Co-optimists squared off against Auckland, representing New Zealand. The Aussies were in a grouping with the Pumas, whose skills were the subject of much fearsome rumour, as well as the hard-tackling Tongans and the speedy Papuans. In another pool, the Baa-Baas, the tough Koreans, the hardy Samoans and the huge Eagles were in a group with popular but unlucky Thailand. The new structure called for a sudden death elimination for the team that came bottom in each pool. There was certain to be ferocious scrabbling during the first day's play to make sure of a place in either the cup or plate quarter-finals.

Hong Kong's legions of sporting spies were soon sending in progress reports from countries where they made business trips. The Barbarians had a strong team, according to exciting reports coming out of Britain, news which was not exactly unexpected of one of the most flamboyant sides ever to take the field. After all, they included five Lions. Fiji left their islands with a blunt statement from their coach, Rupeni Ravonu. "We'll be playing to win," he announced. There was no surprise in that, either. Co-optimists were aiming to do well, said skipper Andy Irvine. But there were dangers aplenty, he added thoughtfully. Like Fiji and Australia and Auckland and the Barbarians. And don't forget Canada and the Eagles and Tonga and the Pumas, he added. Korea wasn't messing about, either, said a Hong Kong textile man who came back from a business trip to Pusan to say that the squad from Seoul would include four battle-hardened soldiers. Japan was going into training in determined style, said reports from Tokyo. They had won the Asian XVs championships and wanted to bring home the Sevens cup as well. Muscat could provide some shocks, said an oil man back home in Hong Kong from the Middle East. They had won the Gulf Sevens and were a speedy and dangerous Sevens squad. What about the American Eagles? Nobody knew much about them except that they were very big and very fast.

Right: No, the ball isn't coming from an Argentinian supporter in the grandstand. It just looks that way as Pumas and Barbarians compete for possession.

Below: An Eagle flies high to evade a Japanese tackler during the 1981 preliminaries. It was, remember ardent fans, one of the best games of that tournament.

"Jack Johnston must have some friends in high places," said one spectator in the stands as he furled his umbrella, stripped off his oilskins, took off his pullover and relaxed in a T-shirt bearing the Sevens logo. Regular fans cast their eyes heavenward and looked in some astonishment at blue skies. As they basked in the sunshine they reflected that the Union chief's appeal to the weatherman had not fallen on deaf ears. The rugby the crowd watched was as brilliant as the weather. Sure enough, Hong Kong went down 34-6 to Fiji. But then the Colony side came raging back onto the field to trounce Japan, mop up the field with Malaysia and down

Jubilant Tongans pretend to throw back the Plate they have just won to Hongkong Banker John Boyer. But the Islanders were joking; they were dead serious about taking the trophy home to show how they had competed with the best players in the world.

Next pages: Andy Ripley of the Barbarians takes off with his fabulous turn of speed that left even the legendary flying Fijians far behind.

Muscat. Hong Kong had won their way into the Cup quarter-finals. It was almost as astonishing a reverse as the weather. "Hong Kong Heroes" screamed the Post in glee. Fiji pulled off a feat equally phenomenal. That first day, they ran up 100 points in their games. The only points scored against them were six racked up by Hong Kong. In other pools, Canada surged into a convincing win over a lacklustre and dismal Auckland side. The Kiwis had none of the glamour or glory that had made their nation world champions. Korea gave the Baa-Baas a nasty jolt, leading 8-6 at the half before the Britons came storming back on the field to end up 26-8 winners. The Wallabies jumped all over the Pumas, but then those sparkling Tongans gave the Australians a shock before the Down Under champions went on to win 16-8.

By Sunday, the weatherman still keeping up his good behaviour, the Football Club stadium was jampacked. "You couldn't have squeezed in another body," said one good-humoured spectator. "You could hardly lift your beer can." Most of the big crowd were too busy clapping to worry about food or drink. Because, all were to agree later that day, it was the best Sevens ever, a day of sparkling, magnificent sport and spectacle. The battle for the Plate saw some gripping matches and ended with Tonga, after a devastating 22-0 win over Auckland, facing Japan. The final was a see-saw battle with first Japan soaring ahead, then Tonga romping into the lead, then Japan fighting grimly back until the popular Islanders clinched victory.

The Cup...! There was drama piled on excitement. For cliff-hanging minutes it looked as though the boys from the Prairies and Rocky Mountains would snatch victory from the Fijians. But the Islanders just managed to scramble home. Then the Pumas pressed hard the Barbarians and the English team had to give their all. The Co-Optimists and the Aussies coasted home, leaving the top four seeded teams to face each other in a bruising battle for supremacy. Fiji and Barbarians provided a head-to-head clash more noted for tactics than excitement. Those dashing brothers Ella spun their magic ball-playing into an Aussie victory over the Scots. So Australia and the Barbarians faced each other for a final. It was going to be a great game, the wise men on the stands muttered, but the green-and-gold would get the glory. So it appeared. The Ellas did their thing and scored a family try but at the half the Barbarians led 6-4. The Baa-Baas started the second half determined to keep possession and deny the ball to the classy Aussie backs. The ball was carried up and down the field. Barbarians scored. Then the Aussies did it again. If they got their hands on the ball, it would be a do-or-die attempt to carry the ball through the Baa-Baa line and snatch victory. The final whistle prevented that and the Barbarians had made history. It was their first appearance at the Sevens and they were plodding with weary delight off the field as holders of the Cup. It meant they were the best team of the Tournament. And that meant that on this day they were the best Sevens team in the world.

Competitions — 1981

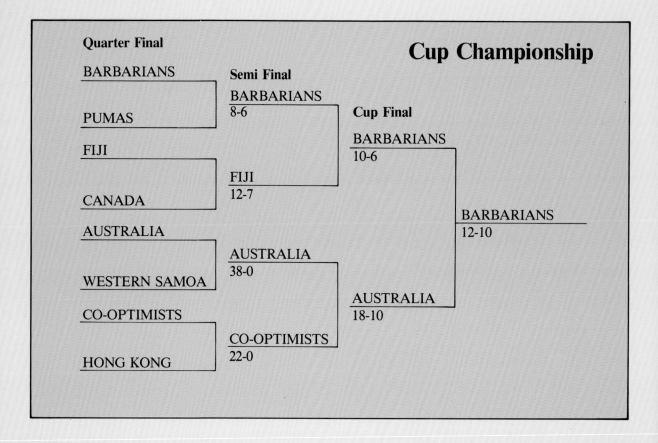

Cup Championship

Quarter Final

BARBARIANS

PUMAS

FIJI

CANADA

AUSTRALIA

WESTERN SAMOA

CO-OPTIMISTS

HONG KONG

Semi Final

BARBARIANS
8-6

FIJI
12-7

AUSTRALIA
38-0

CO-OPTIMISTS
22-0

Cup Final

BARBARIANS
10-6

AUSTRALIA
18-10

BARBARIANS
12-10

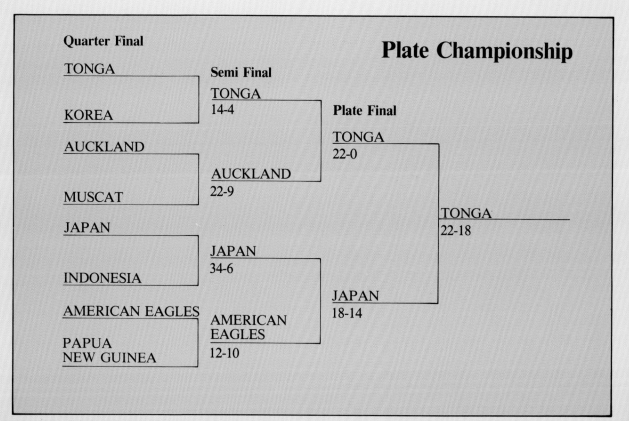

Plate Championship

Quarter Final

TONGA

KOREA

AUCKLAND

MUSCAT

JAPAN

INDONESIA

AMERICAN EAGLES

PAPUA
NEW GUINEA

Semi Final

TONGA
14-4

AUCKLAND
22-9

JAPAN
34-6

AMERICAN
EAGLES
12-10

Plate Final

TONGA
22-0

JAPAN
18-14

TONGA
22-18

Players — 1981

American Eagles
Timothy O'Brien
Bill Baldwin
Arthur Ward
Denis Shanagher
Steve Gray
John Fowler
Tommy Smith
Steve Finkel
Mike Purcell

Auckland (New Zealand)
Ivan Waterson
Steve McCulloch
Kevin Boyle
Bill Preston
Barry Hitchcock
Iain Abercrombie
Mike Mills
Graeme Halse
Richard Falwasser

Australia
Gary Pearse
Chris Roach
Michael O'Connor
Glen Ella
John Maxwell
Mark Ella
Brendan Moon
Roger Gould
Mitchell Cox

Barbarians
Andy Ripley
Peter Wheeler
Nigel Pomphrey
Brymnor Williams
Gareth Williams
Clive Woodward
Gary Pearce
Nick Preston
Les Cusworth
Geoff Windsor-Lewis (M)

Canada
Spence McTavish
Garry Hirayama
Paul Monaghan
John Billingsley
Hans De Goede
Jim Donaldson
Gary Grant
Rob Greig
Ro Hindson
Mike Luke (M)

Co-Optimists (Scotland)
Alan Lawson
Keith Robertson
Andy Irvine
Eric Paxton
Alex Brewster
Roger Baird
Mike Biggar
John Beattie
Ian Forsyth
Fred Mcleod (M)

Fiji
Viliame Ratudradra
Rupeni Ravonu
Iokimi Finau
Ilami Lutumailagi
Paula Waisake
Esala Labalaba
Senivalati Laulau
Dominiko Manaseitava
Aliposo Waqaliti

Hong Kong
Jon Jenkins
Willie Roxburgh
Greg Knight
Dave Duffus
Chris Wynn-Potts
Charles Yeomans
Phil Stavely
Jeff James
John Heptonstall
Peter Duncan (M)

Indonesia
Bob Marsh
Mark Bambridge
Richard Edwards
Alistair Speirs
Tommy Nakamura
Harry Bowman
Alain-Pierre Mignon
Stuart Murray
I. Hughes

Japan
Kazuhiko Honjo
Nobufumi Tanaka
Yoshimitsu Konishi
Hideo Toshima
Fukimi Kanaya
Michihito Chida
Tsuyoshi Fujita
Hiraki Kawachi
Takashi Ito
Hisashi Yokoi (M)

Korea
Hang Park-Gi
Sak Jung-Hyung
Ho Song-Youn
Hee Lee-Jei
Hu Choi-Young
Soo You-Jea
Ho Kim-Sang
Ho Han-Dong
Chen Moon-Young
Ohk Shon Du (M)

Malaysia
Jagjit Singh Bhatt
Lim Say Tee
Zukifli Yacob
Jalil Burhan
Mohd Moor
Tan Ewe Hock
Zukiply Aziz
Kamal Abdullah
Boon Hoon Chee

Muscat
Patrick Sweetnam
John O'Connor
Michael Bennett
James Berry
John Holtby
Adrian Walker
James Gibson
Anthony Pusinelli
David Winter

Papua New Guinea
Lucas Sena
Soiat Williams
Paiwa Bogela
Sab Doiwa
John Pulo
Martin Bingeding
Mike Sere
Titna Pitalai
Alf. Yaya (M)

Pumas (Argentina)
Juan Pablo Piccardo
Marcelo Loffreda
Tomas Petersen
Javier Perez Cobo
Daniel Baetti
Gabriel Travaglini
Rafael Madero
Hugo Porta
Ernesto Ure

Singapore
Ong Poñ Hua
Andrew Chin
David Quek
Chooi Kam Kong
Song Kooh Poh
Lim Khoon Huat
Frank Kwok
Alfred Lee
Buzari Kyat

Sri Lanka
Len De Silva
William Epaarachchi
Kolitha Gunatileke
Saman Jayasinghe
Chris P. Aboyagunawardena
Bharatha Hegoda
Angelo Wickremaratne
Hisham Abdeen
Summa Navaratnam (M)

Thailand
Boonlert Kanchanachongkol
Pornsak Bhandhusidh
Somsak Puekpan
Pramote Sangkakul
Chachaval Thanvarachorn
Pitaya Terbahntern
Suvit Lamsam
Sataya Thepbanterng
Charuay Polprasert

Tonga
Viliami Pone Fotu
Feleti Moala
Pohahau Palu
Semist Faleafa
Sitani Hala'ufia
Kulikefu Lomu
Viliami Moala'eua
Foukimoana Ma'afu
Malakai Pulumu

Western Samoa
Arona Palamo
Taufusi Salesa
Andrew Leavasa
Paul Grey
Osofua Patu
Feausiga Sililoto
Faaniniva Ropati
Ropati Tafuna'i
Toma Aleni

Invitation Sevens

Spectators

Question: Who plays in the Hong Kong Sevens?
Answer: Almost everyone.
Question: Who goes to watch the games?
Answer: Everyone who isn't playing.

Or so it seems. Because every year since 1976 the crowds going to the annual rugby tournament have been getting larger. In 1976, an estimated 3,000 went to the one-day competition. In 1980, when drenching rain turned the Football Club ground into a vast aquatic playground, 9,000 braved the downpour. In 1981, more than 10,500 squeezed into the narrow Happy Valley Stadium and hundreds more were disappointed and turned away because there was just no space. By 1982, the first year that the Sevens were hosted over the hill in Sookunpoo, there were 15,000 watching. And in 1984 the turnstiles clicked 16,000 times on the Saturday and on the Sunday an estimated 21,000 entered the grounds to see the thrilling finals. The 1985 Tournament saw the same level of spectator interest.

The Sevens are the closest thing Hong Kong has to a Mardi Gras. It's a friendly, extroverted, gathering of the Hong Kong clans, a fiesta of fun as well as football. Although Hong Kong is a big

Previous page: In good thirst and good voice, Hong Kong's Welsh community, rugby lovers to a man, brandish their lucky leek, pour a beer and raise their voices in song.

city of 5.5 million people, it is crammed into a small area and the Sevens sometimes seem more like a village fete where everyone knows everybody else rather than a major international sporting tournament. This mixture of local carnival and world competition gives the weekend a unique flavour. So does the presence of the extended international rugby family. For the world rugby community, the Sevens are also a rare chance for a convivial get-together. Usually, meetings of rugby players are one-on-one occasions. All Blacks may see Lions during a tour of Britain. Frenchmen talk to Australians when they go Down Under. Tokyo RFU officials can swap anecdotes with Welshmen during a tour of Japan. But when do Canadian rugby lovers get to talk to Tongans? Or Sri Lankan forwards to Korean backs. Or Scots to Samoans, Americans to Malaysians, Irish full-backs to Singaporean forwards? Nowhere except at the Sevens. And what other figures ever get to talk to the keen players from the islands of the Solomons, the fanatical backs from the hills of New Guinea and the Thais, who seldom go on tour. Never? Except in Hong Kong every Spring. The annual gathering is the only event which brings rugby players, officials and fans from all over the world together in one place at one time. It is the League of Nations of rugbydom, the World Court of the game. It is also a unique and prized opportunity for some of the younger rugby-playing nations of

the world to match their untested skills with the well-honed talents of the giants.

But, above all else, for the spectators it is a weekend of tension-packed excitement mixed with affable companionship.

It's a family weekend. Fathers stagger into the stadium burdened with immense picnic hampers complaining that they have enough food to feed the Lions on a world tour. Loaves of bread, vacuum flasks of curries, piles of fruit, bowls of salad, stacks of sandwiches that could tower over

the 50ft goalposts, steaming containers of coffee... there's always more than enough because between games friends that one hasn't seen since the previous year's Sevens press through the crowds to say hullo and have a bite and a drink and there's likely to be some visiting stranger nearby who looks hungry. "What about the other couple with you?" Oh, they're from New Zealand. We met them here at the Sevens in 1979 and since then we all come back to see each other in Hong Kong every couple of years.

It's a fun weekend. After-game celebrations are almost as important a part of the rugby tradition as is the play on the field and the Hong Kong Sevens weekend is no exception to this hallowed rule. While the players are under strict orders to get early nights and plenty of sleep before the two crucial days of play, no such regulations inhibit the spectators. For the bar owners of Wanchai, just a mile away from the stadium, the Sevens heralds a brief period when the streets where Suzie Wong once lived echo happily to the strains of old rugby songs.

While Scotland of the Borderers has its patron saint in St Andrew and the homeland of the Barbarians is said to be guarded by St George,

Left: Not all spectators are ardent!

Below: The march-past of the players brings them, and the rugby, closer to the spectators.

Umbrellas sprout like mushrooms when the spring rains threaten.

Old Hong Kong hands joke that they are looked over and their interests cared for by St. Michael. Or, more factually, San Miguel. For many years, San Miguel was the only beer brewed in Hong Kong and generations of rugby players grew up with the familiar drink. Now, the Danish-based Carlsberg is also made in Hong Kong and both brews, as well as Lowenbrau, are sold at the Sevens. They are dispensed in gigantic quantities. The thirst of the spectators is as formidable a part of the Sevens tradition as the Fijian pack in full cry down the field. In 1984, vendors at the stadium sold 25,000 pints of beer. Not to mention 12,500 glasses of wine. For those with a taste for harder stuff, whisky, gin and mixed drinks are also on sale. But there is little problem with alcohol at the Sevens. The quantities consumed may be considerable, the thirsts rivalling those of camels after a trans-Sahara trek, but the behaviour is almost invariably jovial, friendly, affable. It's a time for enjoyment for all.

Increasingly every year, there is a welcome international feel to the festival. From the Gulf come a band of fanatics dressed in red-and-white keffiyas, the traditional Arab headgear. They are a colourful group of fans who every year see

Muscat, Dubai or Bahrain go down fighting. How many come to Hong Kong just for the Sevens? It's impossible to say. Hundreds, certainly, from all over the world. By the second year of the Tournament, back in 1977, sizeable groups of Fijian followers were lining up to buy tickets to fly the 14,350 mile round trip to Hong Kong for the rugby. Every year, their number grows. By 1978, Thailand's players were already arriving with 50 keen supporters in tow and at least 20 expatriates from Indonesia that same year decided that a business trip to Hong Kong to coincide with the Sevens was a sudden necessity. Since then, keen rugby followers, non-participating players and officials have followed their teams to Hong Kong. After a couple of years of this, wives decided that what was good enough for their husbands was certainly good enough for them, and a Hong Kong Spring visit is now firmly on the family calendar in rugby homes all over the world. In addition to a weekend of rugby and good-fellowship, the ladies find added attraction in Hong Kong's fame as the shopping centre of the world, a fine way to spend the time when they weary of talk of sport and sportsmen. Cathay Pacific booking staff in Vancouver and Brisbane, London and Bahrain,

Bangkok and Jakarta, are plied with the same sort of questions months in advance of the event. People want to confirm their seats on aircraft that will get them to Kai Tak in time to cross Hong Kong's Fragrant Harbour to get to the Sevens on the Island. The visitors tend to be lost in the crowds on the stands because the likelihood is that they are watching the games with friends or family and in the cosmopolitan international community of Hong Kong, anyone from anywhere tends to melt away in the mob. The only group that stands out are the Middle Easterners, mostly expatriates working in the Gulf, whose headdresses, waving flags and chants are hard to overlook.

The people who crowd the stands at Sookunpoo are, above all, eager to take part in what must be one of the greatest sporting spectaculars in the world. They do so in a setting that must be unique; on a hill behind them, probably unnoticed by 95 percent of the crowd, is a small memorial to another sporting event, the disastrous fire at nearby Happy Valley race track

which left hundreds dead in a 1906 tragedy. The green hills and wooded slopes with their echoing bird calls make the crowded skyscrapers of downtown Hongkong seem far more than a mere mile away.

In this setting, a tradition has grown over the years that stresses the feeling of goodwill and good sportsmanship above the importance of results. Winning is important, certainly. But to the people who watch the Hong Kong Sevens, to the thousands of good-natured followers who fill the stands to cheer for every side that takes the field, the most telling feelings of the two days of unequalled rugby are those of fun and friendship.

Below: Even the head-gear is unique in Hong Kong.

Next pages: All eyes on the ball, massed spectators in the stands follow one of the many gripping moments during a game.

Next pages insert right: Honorary Bedouins, the Bahraini backers fly all the way from the Gulf every year to barrack for their team. The ardent expatriates in Arab head-dress are popular with the crowds. The team always does well and plays sparkling rugby.

Next pages insert left: An ardent fan cheers. For what? For whom? The Sevens is a fiesta to give voice to enthusiasm.

1982

With hundreds of disappointed enthusiasts being turned away from the gates of the Football Club stadium in 1981, the Union decided to look elsewhere for a venue for the seventh Sevens. They did not have far to cast their eyes. Just over a wooded ridge from Happy Valley lies another canyon cutting into the mountains that make up the jagged spine of Hong Kong Island and at the head of the tight, narrow valley is nestled the Hong Kong Government Stadium. Providing twice the seating space of the Football Club ground and all the facilities needed to stage a major tournament, the Stadium was the logical choice for a new home for the championship. But could the Union get it for an entire weekend? After negotiations with Hong Kong Government sports administrators and other sporting bodies, groups which showed the best of sporting fellowship and raised no objections to rugby having its glorious two days, the Stadium was secured.

But then there were other problems. New Zealand, without doubt one of the handful of great nations in the rugby world, had always

Opposite page: An American Eagle is about to come down to earth with a thump, skillfully taken in full flight by a Gulf tackler.

taken a somewhat offhand attitude to the Sevens. Their national union had declined time and again to send a national team to Hong Kong and had "given" the much-desired invitation to the event to the provincial team which won the Kiwis' own national Sevens contest. There had been discussion in Hong Kong and seemingly endless correspondence between the host organisation and the rugby administrators in New Zealand. Finally, the Hong Kong Union dropped what was to many a bombshell; New Zealand would not be invited to send a team. This was no easy decision and one taken with a great deal of heartache and regret. Within the Hong Kong Union Committee, argument had been intense. But the decision had been taken. The Kiwis were told it was not felt that an invitation could be extended. Participation in 1981 had been lacklustre. It had certainly not been up to the standard expected of an All Black side. The vast potential that New Zealand could exert in improving and enhancing the Sevens Tournament was being squandered by the policy of sending a club team to play in Hong Kong. The decision was bitterly received in New Zealand. In

Welsh international Clive Rees goes for goal in a 1982 clash with the Canadians.

The Borderers struggle against a very determined Tonga side in this needle Group C match.

Hong Kong, many ardent Kiwi rugby followers were dismayed that the Sevens would not see a New Zealand team on the field. But other Hong Kong Kiwis [this writer included] strongly backed the decision not to invite a club team. If New Zealand was invited, they should send a national team which could proudly wear the famous All Black shirts. And so the Tournament went on without one of the finest rugby nations being represented.

On every other front, however, it was looking like being yet another sensational year. With the Kiwis out, there was also debate about whether a national "home" side would be coming for another ardent group of Hong Kong fans. The Co-optimists were not returning and the tartan army that make up such a large percentage of Hong Kong's expatriate community, and rugby fans, were wondering for whom they would cheer. Then came news that a team of Scottish Borderers would come from the clubs where Sevens were first played a century before. The police band prepared to pump up their pipes when word arrived that the Scots team would include five internationals. The Barbarians were not going to concede anything to their northern cousins and were heading back with a rugged pack. "We're here to entertain," maintained their star fly-half, Les Cusworth. They were also in town to pick up the championship cup for the second time, some of his team mates added.

Hong Kong once again faced a tough draw; the Aussies were in their pool and this year the big men from Down Under were not planning to come second to anyone in any of the matches. They were back with one aim — to win the Cup.

In the same pool were the Canadians and it was a measure of how they had improved at Sevens in the years they had been doing friendly battle in the competition that they were now regarded as a team worthy of facing the Wallabies. It looked, commented one Hong Kong fan, that the home team would be in the unenviable position of the legendary mouse watching the elephants dance; in acute danger of being squashed during the festivities. Korea sent a fleet squad of tough tacklers, Samoa dispatched a team said to contain a few surprises, the American Eagles came joking that they were ready to soar with a fleet Nigerian-born three-quarter and an imposing lumberjack who quipped that he was included to cut down the opposition. There were doubts if the Tongans would even arrive; their homeland had been hit by a devastating hurricane but the delightful, smiling Pacific players were determined not to miss out on the festival. The Japanese squad was said to be experienced and a tough nut to crack. The Fijians were sending some of their fastest high-flyers and the Pumas were dispatching virtually a brand-new team which contained only two players from the previous year.

A race for the line.

Jack Johnston's contacts with the weathermen seemed to be paying off again because the sun was shining brightly on Saturday, March 27, as thousands of spectators began filing into the new Sevens ground. Nothing, however, could outshine the performances on the field. The Barbarians, Scottish Borderers, Australia and Fiji — the expected Big Four — all made it into the semi-finals. But not without some surprises, notably a near-upset when the Tongans had the Borderers groggy and on the ropes for much of a game which saw the Scots desperately battling to scramble home with a 10-9 win. Once again, it was a year of upsets and magnificent performances by Malaysia, the American Eagles and Thailand who showed that their annual

Scotland's Eric Paxton fends off Peter Wheeler of the Barbarians.

pilgrimage to Hong Kong was improving dramatically the way they played the game. But it was Tonga, a pack of sparkling players, who were this year's favourites. When they clashed with Fiji, the perennial sweethearts of the Tournament, in the Cup championship quarter-final, the crowd roared itself hoarse for both sides. Fiji won, 8-4.

Hong Kong got knocked out of the Cup by crushing defeats inflicted by Australia and the vastly-improved Canadians. They dashed through the first elimination bout for the Plate championship only to be knocked out by Japan. The Plate final was a game to remember. Korea, fit, disciplined, fast and tough-tackling, played brilliantly. They smashed down the field to a 32-6 victory over once-mighty Japan and their display brought ovation after roaring ovation from an appreciative crowd. It was another example of how a side had improved with practice gained after year after grinding year at the Sevens.

Meanwhile, there were dramatic clashes as the fields narrowed for the Cup. Baa-Baas and Scots came face to formidable face and in a thrilling game played at furious pace the Borderers ran out winners. Then those old friendly foes Australia and Fiji crashed head-on in a contest in which spectacle combined with tension and went on into extra time. The superfit Australians were exhausted when they clinched a 10-6 victory. After two days of slam-bang, fast-running rugby,

the 14 men who took to the field for the final game should have been running in a daze of weariness. If so, it certainly didn't show. The Cup final was dazzling. The Scots, said one admiring Englishman, came storming into the game like old border cattle raiders used to come down into England — so fast you couldn't catch them. After kick-off, the Borderers got the ball and had scored before the Aussies had even touched the pigskin. The Australians made it even. Another try to the Borderers left the Scots leading 12-10 at the half and the final result as unpredictable as ever. The crowd, thrilled by rugby the like of which the world has seldom seen, were spurred to frantic cheering. The roar from the stands was non-stop as Aussie scored again, then the Scots were on the attack when the final whistle signalled an end to the 1982 Sevens and the green-and-gold jerseys of the Australian winners were waved in elated victory. Ecstatic Aussies in the crowd sung Waltzing Matilda. And a fair number of Scots were singing with them to mark the end of what all agreed was a magnificent weekend.

All told, everyone was to agree at the subsequent celebrations that last long through the night, the best team had won. But they were not the only winners, argued the SCM Post in an editorial praising the organisers and the move to Sookunpoo. The Tournament had been an outstanding success. Rugby was the winner.

Competitions — 1982

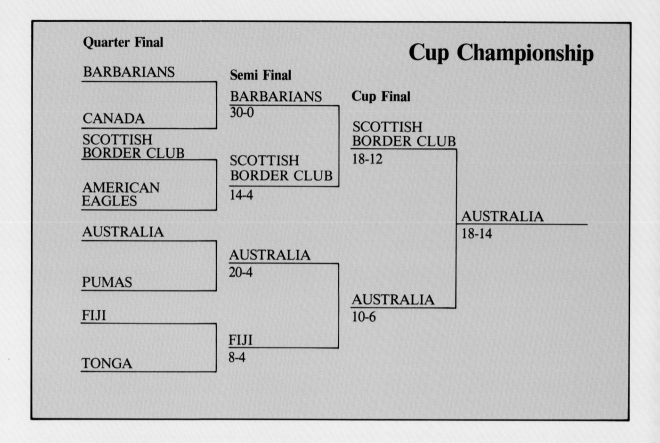

Cup Championship

Quarter Final

BARBARIANS

CANADA

SCOTTISH BORDER CLUB

AMERICAN EAGLES

AUSTRALIA

PUMAS

FIJI

TONGA

Semi Final

BARBARIANS
30-0

SCOTTISH BORDER CLUB
14-4

AUSTRALIA
20-4

FIJI
8-4

Cup Final

SCOTTISH BORDER CLUB
18-12

AUSTRALIA
10-6

AUSTRALIA
18-14

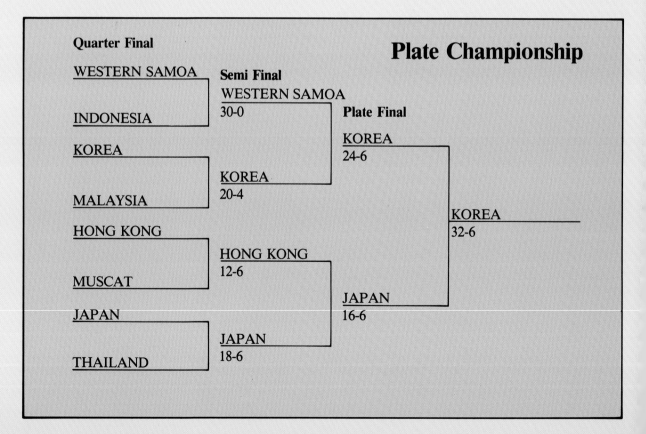

Plate Championship

Quarter Final

WESTERN SAMOA

INDONESIA

KOREA

MALAYSIA

HONG KONG

MUSCAT

JAPAN

THAILAND

Semi Final

WESTERN SAMOA
30-0

KOREA
20-4

HONG KONG
12-6

JAPAN
18-6

Plate Final

KOREA
24-6

JAPAN
16-6

KOREA
32-6

Players — 1982

American Eagles
Steve Gray
Mike Purcell
Chimere Okezi
Denis Shanagher
David Bateman
Gary Lambert
Steve Finkel
John Fowler
Tommy Smith
Keith Seaber (M)

Australia
John Maxwell
Chris Roche
Gary Pearse
Michael O'Connor
Glen Ella
Peter Lucas
Brendan Moon
Qele Ratu
Mark Ella
Peter Falk (M)

Barbarians
John O'Driscoll
Nigel Melville
Stuart Barnes
Clive Rees
S. Jones
Eddie Butler
Les Cusworth
Peter Wheeler
Clive Woodward
Geoff Windsor-Lewis (M)

Brunei
Barry Moore
James Wee Kim Kheng
David Toyad Yong
Kenneth Swift
Rhodri Johns
Aji Bin Hussin
Lawrie Harris
Barry Sayer
Cliff Berry
Peter Thomas (M)

Canada
Ro Hindson
Evan Jones
Paul Monaghan
Hans De Goede
Dennis Sinnott
Jamie Hawthorn
Brooke Smith
Garry Hirayama
Dave Tucker
Alan Rees (M)

Fiji
Lepani Tagicakibau
Esala Labalaba
Senivalati Laulau
Marika Nasegai
Aliposo Waqaliti
Sela Gutugutuwai
Ilami Lutumailagi
Marika Toga
Dominiko Manaseitava
Tevita Rabuli (M)

Hong Kong
Jon Jenkins
Charles Gregory
Willie Roxburgh
Michael Bracher
Chris Wynn-Potts
Tony Tyler
Charles Yeomans
Norrie Rae
Phil Stavely
Peter Duncan (M)

Indonesia
Alistair Speirs
Harry Bowman
David Chapman
Steven Simpson
Paul Thomas
Alain-Pierre Mignon
Maksum Suhaidi
Robert Mason
Peter Merrett
David Parry (M)

Japan
Yuji Matsuo
Michihito Chida
Kazuhiko Honjo
Yasuharu Kawase
Fukumi Kanaya
Hikaru Kawaji
Hideo Tojima
Yoshimitsu Konishi
Takashi Ito
Shigetaka Mori (M)

Korea
Ho Song-Youn
Soo You-Jea
Tock Cho-Yong
Chen Moon-Young
Il Song-No
Sak Jung-Hyung
Hu Choi-Young
Hwan Hwang-II
Ho Han-Dong
Ohk Shon-Du (M)

Malaysia
Ruslan Siru
Marc Boon Hoon Chee
Zulkiply Aziz
Mohd Noor Amin
Yassin Said
Lim Say Tee
Zulkifli Yacob
Tan Ewe Hock
Lee Wen Bin
Pang Kong Ying (M)

Muscat
James Gibson
Michael Bennett
Steven Robertson
John O'Connor
Adrian Walker
Allan Malcolm
James Kelly
James Berry
Gareth Jones
Christopher Morton (M)

Papua New Guinea
Sab Doiwa
John Pulo
Martin Bingeding
Lucas Sena
Soiat Williams
Elisa Maira
Paiwa Bosela
Jack Takavis

Pumas
Tomas Ricardo Landajo
Tomas Andres Peterson
Juan Pablo Piccardo
Jorge Miguel Gauweloose
Guillermo Paz
Guillermo Cesar Lorenzo
Alejandro Jaime Sartori
Alejandro Marcelo Schiavio
Gonzalo Repetto
Lino Perez (M)

Scottish Border Club
Bob Hogarth
Jim Renwick
Eric Paxton
Roger Baird
Gary Callendar
Keith Robertson
Iain Paxton
John Rutherford
Derek White
Bert Duffy (M)

Singapore
Buzari Bin Kayat
Colin Lee
Alan Wee
Song Koon Poh
Andrew Chin
Mohd Rashid
Frank Kwok
Sairi Osman
Lim Chye Lai
John Burgess (M)

Sri Lanka
Saman Jayasinghe
Bharatha Hegoda
Len De Silva
Nihal Gunaratne
S. Sritharan
Hubert Rayan
H.K. Sisira
Nalin De Silva
Subramaniam Sujanthakumar
Summa Navaratnam (M)

Thailand
Suvit Lamsam
Songtham Allapach
Songsak Malithong
Yongsil Rattanayongkijkorn
Boonlert Kanchanachongkol
Somsak Puekpan
Pramote Sangkakul
Chachaval Thanvarachorn
Sataya Thepbunterng
Madhana Lansaad (M)

Tonga
Sitani Hala'ufia
Pohahau Palu
Feleti Moala
Viliami Lutua
Donald Tevi
Suiti Leilani
Paea Moala
Alamoni Liava'a
Tu'ikolovatu Halafihi
Viliami H. Petelo (M)

Western Samoa
Taufusi Salesa
Taumaloto Loi
Ma'afala Lima
Feausina Sililoto
Faafiti Simaile Siliga
Ropati Tafunai
Lomitusi Sasi
Alatimu Lese
Osofua Patu
Tapusatele K. Tuatagaloa (M)

Press

Nobody loves the Sevens more than the press. The Tournament not only provides sparkling copy and brilliant opportunities for photographs, it also gives sporting reporters from all over the world a chance to rub shoulders with each other and talk to the world's top players and officials. It provides top scribes like Ian Robertson of The Sunday Times with the rare opportunity to speak to Lucas Sena of Port Moresby, a player of whom the authoritative writer had never heard before he came to the 1982 Sevens. Robertson's millions of regular readers were soon to read of Sena and the other likeable Papua New Guineans. It's that kind of story that spreads knowledge from the little-known backwaters of rugby into the great capitals of the rugby world that is one of the most desirable spin-offs of the Sevens.

Peter Bush, ace lensman of New Zealand Truth, is arguably the doyen of the world's rugby photographers. He has been to more international games than any All Black who ever lived, travelling the well-beaten jet highways of the international touring teams and the lesser-known byways taken by New Zealand club sides overseas. Nothing in his career has excited him as

much as the Sevens. Not even being tear-gassed while covering a riot outside a stadium in Capetown or being arrested by security police while on a train going through Hungary when he was returning from a rugby visit to Rumania. "Unbelievable," he said as a score of teams jogged around Sookunpoo in 1983 and the photographer, known to rugby players around the globe as The Bushman, frantically wielded his ferocious array of bazooka-like lenses.

Hong Kong's own press corps, an army of cameramen from more than 70 daily newspapers, are also appreciative of the Sevens. The photographers from the Chinese papers may not know much about the finer points of rugby, but they are experts when it comes to getting good

Bottom: TV watchers in every rugby nation see their teams in action.
Below: Newspapers from every major rugby playing nation in Asia and the Pacific have their men at the games.

Opposite page: Heads covered, lenses protected, cameramen continue to work through the showers.

The doyen of the world's rugby photographers, Peter Bush of New Zealand Truth, takes a break between games. Weighed down with equipment weighing more than 20 lbs and running the length of the field many times each match, Bush reckons to lose five pounds over the Sevens weekend. But he keeps coming back for gruelling punishment every year. Why? "It's magic," he says, ranking the Sevens the most photogenic rugby he has seen in 30 years of covering the game in every corner of the world.

pictures and they rate the Sevens tops for action shots. The annual coverage of spectacular sporting prints that appear in the Chinese press in Hong Kong has done much to raise local interest in the competition and to attract to the stadium an ever-increasing number of Hong Kong sports-lovers who want entertainment as well as enlightenment. They get both.

The reporters and photographers who follow rugby balls around the world, men like Robertson and Bush, are members of a small but distinguished band for whom the game is a labour of love as well as what they see as the best way in the world to make a living. Walking encyclopaedias of rugby, they are probably the best judges on earth of what makes the game tick. So their opinions are worth considering. Wrote Robertson: "In the heart of Hong Kong, surrounded by skyscrapers, the Sevens provided a feast of exotic rugby. This Tournament is the biggest and best Sevens tournament in the world. The list of household names includes a galaxy of stars." Adds Bush: "What can you say? Marvellous photo opportunities. Fantastic setting. Magnificent hospitality. Tremendous stories. Upsets galore. Great, fast, thrilling rugby." He throws his hands wide. "What more could anyone want?"

As it is for the players and the fans, the hallmark of the Sevens is for the visiting heavyweights of the press an enjoyable experience. The respected writer George Mackay of London's Daily Telegraph, one of the major "rugby" newspapers of the world, would like to record some of the doings of journalistic adventurers who journey to Sookunpoo. Unfortunately, he notes wryly, many of the tales are unfit for the pages of a family newspaper. He does remember flying in the splendour of Cathay first class en route to Hong Kong one year, idly spinning his brandy balloon, when a companion recalled that as a boy he had been warned by a teacher against taking too great an interest in rugby. The game would never get him anywhere in life, he had been warned. Sipping luxuriantly, he wondered where his former schoolmaster was at that moment. There are other moments that Mackay, like most visiting pressmen, treasure. "An abiding memory of my first experience at the Sevens came at a post-tournament dinner. There amid the fun and frivolity stood a remarkable trio — a New Zealander, a South Korean and a skirted South Sea Islander — arms around each other's shoulders, faces beaming with emotion, singing along in three mutually incomprehensible languages. That cameo captured the wonderful air of international friendship unique to the Tournament."

No writer has followed the Sevens so closely, written about them so reliably, spoken to so many participants and recorded so faithfully the victories and heartbreaks of the decade as has the veteran Jack Beattie of the South China Morning Post. The affable Scot has been writing rugby for years and swears that the Sevens are, for a sporting scribe, one of the greatest shows on earth.

Back-up for the press comes in a sophisticated computer control room where sports press coordinator William Brown helps puts in the figures. Every match, fresh up-to-the second statistics on teams, results and standings come chattering out of the computer. Reporters vote the service the best they have seen anywhere in world rugby.

Next page: A quiet comment on the weather.

.THAY PACIFIE (7) HONGKONG BA

Left: Like Apaches in ambush in a film from a western movie,
press photographers line the roof of the Football Club.
Newsmen, broadcasters, television crews and film documentary
makers from all over the world come to Hongkong for the
tournament. It has helped to put the eyes of the sporting world
firmly on the Colony for two days of the year.

Above: Long range lenses focussed on the goal line, press
photographers are ready to catch the drama on the grass.

But the reporters and photographers who journey every year to the Government Stadium are not there just for fun. They have a serious, demanding job to do and, until that job is done, despite the well-held image of the hard-drinking newsman, there is little time for festivities. They make up for it, however, when the Tournament is over and they join the other members of the Sevens community — players, officials, organisers, sponsors — at the big farewell banquet. Before then, the typewriters are running hot in the press stand high above the ground. The phones are ringing with calls from Wellington, Sydney, Dubai, Singapore, Suva, Vancouver, Kobe, Seoul and London. Stories are being shouted in a bedlam of a dozen tongues. Messengers are dashing off with rolls of film to process and one little corner of the stadium takes on the lunatic frenzy of stubbed cigarette butts, spilt coffee, lurid language and hurled typewriter ribbons that can be recognised by any newspaperman from any corner of the world as being a reporters' room as deadline approaches.

In the midst of this mental carnage, a cross between civil war and volcanic eruption, are the two men who more than any others help the world to know next morning what has happened at Sookunpoo. David Bell is public relations manager for Swires, the mammoth trading company that controls Cathay Pacific. For a decade, he has been bringing to Hong Kong some of the leading rugby writers and commentators from major publications linked with the sport. Who to invite is a tricky business, and he solves it on the basis of selecting known writers who are knowledgeable about the sport and whose papers have a history of taking an interest in it. It is no easy task to select 25 people from the hundreds of enquiries that organisers receive from all over the world. The press plays a vital, often under-rated role in the Sevens. Nobody can guess how

many people read about the event in newspapers, magazines and books, how many view it on television or listen to broadcasts of the games. Tens of millions, certainly. Hundreds of millions, perhaps. When a reader picks up the Fiji Sun and yells with delight as he sees the team has done well, it is a fellow called Jeff Mann who has helped put the news on the front page on his breakfast table. Mann has been involved in the Sevens for almost the entire life of the tournament and in that time the publicity back-up for press covering the event has reached levels of sophistication seldom seen anywhere in the world. Reporters on the press bench are now accustomed to electronic luxuries like computer print-outs before each game giving vital statistics on players, standings in the Tournament, personal details of all players, the name of the ref and conditions on the pitch. One year, as a laugh, a reporter asked one of Mann's staff what the Solomon Islanders had had for breakfast. A couple of minutes later, back came the accurate answer. The author of this book has covered parliaments and international conferences all over the world. He has never seen an organisation as efficient as the Mann team when it comes to giving the press the facts — fast and accurately — that reporters need to do their job.

Their job is a vital one. It is to tell the folks back home, the television viewers, the radio listeners and the newspaper and magazine readers all over the globe, what has happened over the weekend that the eyes of the rugby world have been rivetted on Hong Kong. By and large, it is a job they do well.

1983

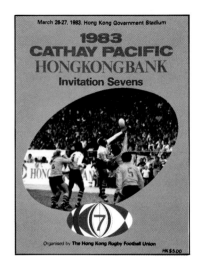

March 26-27, 1983. Hong Kong Government Stadium

**1983
CATHAY PACIFIC
HONGKONGBANK
Invitation Sevens**

Organised by The Hong Kong Rugby Football Union

HK$5.00

It looked like the end of the world. In mid-afternoon on the Saturday of the Sevens, a gigantic black cloud came rolling inexorably down from the north. It blanketed the stadium, hanging ominously in the air a couple of hundred feet above the grass. Suddenly, in the middle of the day, it was literally as black as midnight. The lights were switched on and play continued as players, officials and spectators cast uneasy eyes towards the impenetrable gloom. It was, remarked one worried mother holding two frightened children, like being in a rubbish bin with the lid closed. The atmospheric freak which brought the cloud of doom to Sookunpoo was a unique phenomenon caused by a combination of unusual atmospheric conditions. Whatever the reason, it was a spectacular performance by Mother Nature. If the weather conditions caused people in Hong Kong to think the end was nigh, followers of the home team at the Sevens felt this was just confirmation of what they had already seen happen when Hong Kong was trounced 42-0 by Fiji.

Back at the Government Stadium for the second year, officials had done a lot of behind-the-scenes planning to ensure that events on the stands went as smoothly as they did on the field. The logistics of looking after about 16,000 people each day in one venue were daunting. It was not like a normal sporting event lasting a couple of hours but an all-day occasion during which people had to be fed, cared for and provided with toilets, aid, advice and medical care. Booths for lost children were needed and cover [badly needed, as it turned out] in case of rain. The spectators had to be able to get food and drink and more drink and told what was going on. It was like running a miniature city. There were crowds not only from Hong Kong but from many lands. The infectious spirit of fun and excitement had drawn them to Hong Kong, said Cathay's chairman Duncan Bluck in his welcoming statement. It had gone far beyond Hong Kong's boundaries and the voyagers were very welcome.

Also welcome were a couple of new teams. The Kiwis were back, this time sending a national team following the absence of the Men in Black the previous year. And they were back with a vengeance. They left nobody in any doubt that they were out to win. Although New Zealand

Previous page: Here's mud in your eye! Birds of a feather, they say, flock together. In this case, it's the American Eagles and the New Zealand Kiwis wallowing in company in the 1983 mudbath conditions. Somewhere in the middle, maybe, is the ball.

Churning through the viscous mud, Hong Kong powers to the to the attack gaainst a plucky but bogged-down Malaysian side in one of the exciting 1983 Plate quarter finals.

Arising from the mire like some muddy amphibian, one of the dashing brothers Ella — who can pick which one? — gasps for breath as he rejons play. The relentless Wallaby attack crushed the gallant Tongans in this campaign in the mire.

teams had taken to the Hong Kong fields in all but one of the Sevens, this was the first time an official All Black squad participated. They meant to make their mark. In particular, they meant to remind their Australian cousins from across the Tasman Sea that New Zealand was the Rugby super-power of the Pacific. There was yet another new team from the watery vastness of the great ocean and like the Fijians, Tongans and Samoans, the Solomon Islanders were swiftly to prove themselves crowd pleasers with their light-footed, dazzling pace.

The teams that came to Hong Kong that year had been under the microscope for months. None had been subject to such scrutiny as the All Blacks whose prowess and skills had been debated endlessly. His fellow Kiwis had a lot to learn about Sevens, a different game than the power-packed full XV's game at which they were so proficient, pointed out well-known Hong Kong rugby commentator Jamie Scott. The Samoan squad was an unknown but threatening quantity. Singapore, too, had opted for a number of new faces. Canada had selected a strong contingent. The powerful Eagles team were tipped to be big improvers. The Scots Borderers came without some of their top men; the Sevens date clashed unavoidably with a Scotland vs Barbarians match to mark the opening of the new stand at historic Murrayfield, the home ground of Scottish rugby, where a series to mark the first century of Sevens was being staged. Nobody was forgetting the two most formidable teams; both Fiji and Australia from thousands of miles away cast long shadows over the ground at Sookunpoo.

But the weather was casting shadows of its own. Jack Johnston seemed to have lost his earlier benign influence with Mother Nature which in recent years had worked so well. March

came in wet and rainy and stayed that way. By March 26, Tournament eve, more than 340mm of rain had fallen on Hong Kong that month, 10 times the average for the month. Statistics kept by the Royal Observatory showed it was the wettest March for 99 years. The rain kept coming down. There was no end in sight.

Hong Kong had trained on through the mire to reach peak condition. The squad got on with the work of preparing to meet some prominent opposition. If the weather was gloomy, so were Hong Kong's chances of winning their first game; the luck of the draw had pitted them against mighty Fiji.

For a time it was doubtful that the teams would even meet on the field. Rain came down in endless sheets and the stadium grounds, which had been extensively returfed at heroic efforts by the groundstaff needed urgent attention. The ground was a swamp. Union officials and visiting coaches went out to the stadium and waded through the water. On the Saturday, play was possible. But conditions were worsening as the surface was torn up by sprigs. Would play be possible on the Sunday? Many thought not. Radio stations and newspapers were also deluged — not with rain but with calls from anxious fans. Would the games go on? At 9-30am, under lowering clouds and in dense rain, Jack Johnston called together as many as possible of the team managers. They walked the pitch. Could their players compete in this mud? The answer was unanimous: "Let rugby be played." And rugby was played.

Caked with mud, it was hard to tell the Scottish Borderers and the Tongans apart after the first few minutes of play.

The weather may have been overcast, dull and depressing. The Solomons played dazzling rugby and soared through to the finals of the Plate. Bahrain, the Middle East's representatives, surprised everyone but themselves by putting down Korea and then giving the American Eagles a close run that had the crowd on their feet. The Seven's reputation for upsets was predictably upheld with the seeded Canadian team, much improved though they were, knocked out as Cup contenders by the exhuberant Samoans. The next day, Korea was to defeat them in the Plate final 30-6. But that first day's play, in clinging earth under threatening skies, produced some excellent rugby.

Any chance of Hong Kong gaining glory was ended when Canada beat the home team 8-4 after a desperate game that finished only after a sudden-death try by the North Americans in extra time. Earlier, the mercurial Tongans had gained supremacy in another cliff-hanger of a game to run Hong Kong into the ground 10-8 and put the local men out of the Cup. Still, sitting on the sidelines watching the clash of the titans was recompense enough for any rugby lover because what was to come amid the quagmire was a series of epic battles.

The rain had continued. But nobody took much notice of the appalling weather. There were other attention-grabbing matters happening out on the field glimpsed through the sheets of rain. Samoa knocked out the New Zealanders. Australia put down Samoa. Fiji disposed of Japan 20-0, then the Scots 14-8. And in the gloom, amid the slushy mud, treacherous and slippery, the Big Two came to a thrilling finale providing possibly one of the finest games of Sevens anyone present had ever seen. The Aussies, as many were to affirm, had the stamp of champions. The Fijians possessed their usual flair and skill. But the ball, smeared with the greasy mixture from a field churned into thin barley soup, had a life of its own. It had to be captured rather than merely caught. The electric newcomer David Campese weaved and bolted gracefully down the mud. Mark Ella was injured. Ironically, replacing him on the field was an ex-Fijian player Quele Ratu. Slithering to victory, 14-4, the ecstatic Aussies equalled Fiji's three Sevens victories and the huge Australian contingent amid the 16,000 spectators went mad. At the celebration ball that night, there was only one song. And the Fijians were in full voice as they joined their old friends and adversaries in chorus after chorus of Waltzing Matilda.

Competitions — 1983

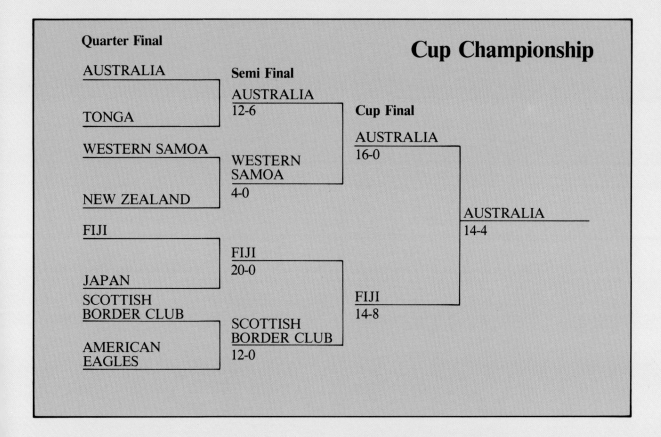

Cup Championship

Quarter Final

AUSTRALIA

TONGA

WESTERN SAMOA

NEW ZEALAND

FIJI

JAPAN

SCOTTISH
BORDER CLUB

AMERICAN
EAGLES

Semi Final

AUSTRALIA
12-6

WESTERN
SAMOA
4-0

FIJI
20-0

SCOTTISH
BORDER CLUB
12-0

Cup Final

AUSTRALIA
16-0

FIJI
14-8

AUSTRALIA
14-4

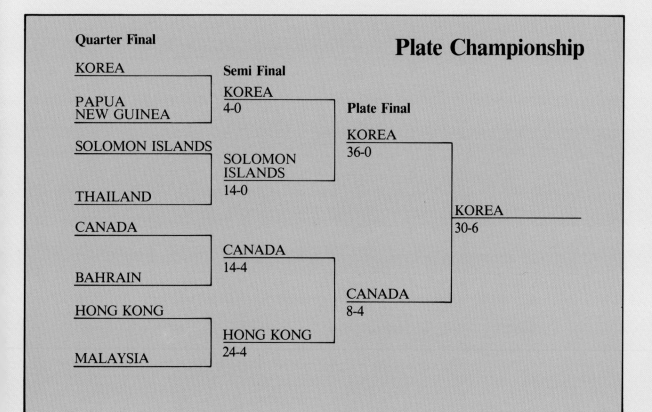

Plate Championship

Quarter Final

KOREA

PAPUA
NEW GUINEA

SOLOMON ISLANDS

THAILAND

CANADA

BAHRAIN

HONG KONG

MALAYSIA

Semi Final

KOREA
4-0

SOLOMON
ISLANDS
14-0

CANADA
14-4

HONG KONG
24-4

Plate Final

KOREA
36-0

CANADA
8-4

KOREA
30-6

Players — 1983

American Eagles
John Fowler
Steve Finkel
Richard Primm
David Bateman
Dick Cooke
Tim O'Brien
Mike Purcell
Willie Jefferson
Denis Shanagher
David Chambers (M)

Australia
John Maxwell
David Campese
Glen Ella
Mark Ella
Peter Lucas
Brendan Moon
Gary Pearse
Qele Ratu
Chris Roche
Peter Falk (M)

Bahrain
Richard Duck
Richard Bevens
Colin Rick
Timothy Downes
Bruce Collins
Timothy Murley
Mark Thompson
Mark Moss
Mike Stapleton
Jim Fitzsimons (M)

Brunei
Lawrie Harris
Barry Moore
Julian Dalzell
Rhodri Johns
Kenneth Swift
D. Bulbeck
D. Jarvis
S. Fox
Iain Stewart
John Williams (M)

Canada
Dennis Sinnott
Ro Hindson
John Billingsley
Ian MacMillan
Mark Wyatt
John Lecky
Jim Donaldson
Spence McTavish
Alan Rees (M)

Fiji
Esala Labalaba
Senivalati Laulau
Dominiko Manaseitava
Sela Gutugutuwai
Aliposo Waqaliti
Ropate Senikuraciri
Severo Kuruduadua
Ilai Koroitamana
Marika Toga
Tevita Rabuli (M)

Hong Kong
Michael Bracher
Willie Roxburgh
Paddy Sweetnam
Charles Yeomans
Andy Stevens
Brian Eastgate
Ian Duguid
Eamonn McManus
Charles Gregory
Peter Duncan (M)

Indonesia
Stefan Smeenk
Robert Mason
Chris Andrews
Robert Lambert
Peter Merrett
Alain-Pierre Mignon
Steven Simpson
Alastair Speirs
Peter Collins

Japan
Hirotaka Ujino
Michihito Chida
Toshiro Yoshino
Kazuhiko Honjo
Yoshimitsn Konishi
Kentato Tsuchiya
Hiraru Kawachi
Toshi Mashiko
Hiroshi Hibino (M)

Korea
Ho Han-Dong
Chen Moon-Young
Ho Song-Youn
Sak Jung-Hyung
Goon Poy-Joung
Kim Hyun
Dong Ahn-Kwang
Young Jung-Kyen
Pil You-Jae
Ohk Shon-Du (M)

Malaysia
Boon Hoon Chee
Sunsubahar Baharuddin
Peter Kwa
Zulkiply Aziz
Ruslan Siru
Yassin Said
Rosly Ahmad
Lim Say Tee
Zainuddin Mohd
Pang Kong Ying (M)

New Zealand
Alan Dawson
Andrew Donald
Richard Fry
Ken Granger
Allan Lindsay
Hika Reid
Glenn Rich
Joe Stanley
Bruce Smith
Bryce Rope (M)

Papua New Guinea
Jack Takavis
Lucas Sena
John Witchurch
Soiat Williams
Sam Antiko
Leo Parua
Martin Bingeding
John Koi
Elsha Maira
Phil Hope (M)

Scottish Border Club
Norman Jackson
Ivor Roy
Keith Murray
Andrew Ker
Bob Hogarth
Eric Paxton
Gary Callander
Derek White
Bobby Cunningham
Arthur Hastie (M)

Singapore
Lim Chye Lai
Amran Mohd
Chee Kum Tong
Henry Lee Yun Kit
Ishak Hassan
Mohd Rashid
David Quek
Frank Kwok
Andrew Chin
Natahar Bava (M)

Solomon Islands
John Bainivalu
Fa'Ako Liolea
Leonard Pugeva
Joe Vilelea
Warren Bao
Josiah Titia
Job Tuhaika
Jeret Beti
Bobby Ramo
Martin Baker (M)

Sri Lanka
Chris Abeyagunawardene
Hisham Abdeen
Nalin de Silva
W. Epparachchi
Len de Silva
Chula Dharmadasa
Rohan Guneratne
Saman Jayasinghe
H.K. Sisira
J. Ratnam (M)

Thailand
Boonlert Kanchanachongkol
Somsak Phuekpan
Sawat Piammanat
Chucheep Kumfung
Suvit Lamsam
Poj Laksanasompong
Pongkasem Leumprapai
Ekkarat Kladpan
Tanin Patamasingh na Ayudhya
Madhana lansaad (M)

Tonga
Fa'onelua Fakaua
Tu'ikolovatu Halafihi
Takai Makisi
Kapelieli Vunipola
Tohi Leha
Ofa Blake
Talai Fifita
'Otenili Pifeleti
'Alamoni Liava'a
Viliami Petelo (M)

Western Samoa
Taufusi Salesa
Ta'i Fong
David Schuster
Pati Maligi
Lolani Lolani
Lomitsui Sasi
Tini Mavaega
Sepe Tupuola
Winston Ryan
Paul Wallwork (M)

Mini Rugby

Mini rugby was born in Hong Kong in 1979. It has proved to be a lusty, healthy baby. By 1980, teams of under-nines were playing demonstration matches as curtain raisers to the Sevens. They proved to be almost as popular as the idolised Fijians, who towered about five feet above some of the boys. Schoolchildren in Hong Kong have probably been getting an informal introduction to rugby since the game first came to the Colony and they were old enough to catch a ball tossed to them on a lawn by a keen father. But on a regular, organised basis, mini rugby made its appearance first in the winter months of 1979 when parents and players at Kowloon and Police clubs got together informally to teach interested boys a few of the finer points of the game.

Today, more than 400 boys take part in regular Sunday morning sessions at the Police Sports Club at Kai Tak, on the playing fields at Stanley Fort, the Hong Kong Football Club, and in Sekkong. It is, says the co-ordinator of mini rugby, Terry Orsler, not only an investment in catching boys young and giving them an interest in the game, but also a lot of fun. And he doesn't mean just for the boys, either. Men like Terry Orsler also get a vast amount of pleasure out of teaching

Previous page and below: Determination written plain on every face, the youngsters take their days of glory on the pitch just as seriously as older players take their own appearances in national colours.

youngsters how to play the game. But the emphasis is not on rules and regulations; the stress is on fun, enjoyment, good fellowship and sportsmanship. In that way, mini rugby is a lot like the Sevens Tournament in which every boy one day hopes to wear the Hong Kong jersey.

Rugby players are made, not born. In Hong Kong, they tend to be made from the age of seven years old, which is the youngest they can take part in organised mini rugby training. The men who every weekend give of their time and

Below: All little boys like the mud. But for the pint-sized heroes of the mini-rugby curtain raisers, it can sometimes be too much of a good thing. In one quagmire year at the Football Club venue anxious mothers and wary coaches had to count heads as the teams emerged from a ruck to make sure that all players had come out of the mud.

patience to put the boys through their enthusiastic paces come from many fields. They may, like Terry Orsler, be policemen who hailed originally from Britain, men who have played as youths at school in their home countries and then for clubs and Hong Kong sides. Or Australian airline pilots. Or Scots bankers. Or Japanese executives. Or New Zealand teachers. Or American writers. In other words, the coaches are typical Hong Kong rugby followers. They don't even have to know a great deal about the more intricate laws of the game; they just have to like to see young people get out and enjoy themselves in good, clean, friendly competition.

One of the greatest boosts that mini rugby ever had in Hong Kong was the demonstration game that some boys played in the 1980 Sevens. That was the year that the pitch was 18 inches under water and the spectacle of the boys wading thigh-deep towards the goal line won the admiration of all sports lovers. Sevens organisers were hesitant about letting the boys play the planned curtain raiser. Jack Johnston, then Chairman of the Union, asked Terry Orsler what he thought. Terry Orsler asked them. The reply could be heard throughout the ground: "PLAY!" they piped in a variety of accents and languages. And play they did, right into the hearts of the crowd. Next year, the boys took their place with other teams in the march past, proudly carrying their own Mini Rugby placard. They won applause as deafening as that given to the adult Hong Kong team. Do the boys like playing at the Sevens? Like it? They love it, maintains Terry Orsler. Where else in the world, he asks, in any sport, can a seven-year-old tread on the same turf on the same day as the international champions? Nowhere. Except in Hong Kong and during the Sevens.

Off the field comes a young warrior. He has learned the most important lesson of the rugby pitch — sportsmanship.

Next pages: In a few short years, mini-rugby – partly funded by money raised by the Sevens — has become a popular event. But through the winter, boys put in hours of practice under the keen eyes of experienced coaches who are building Hong Kong's rugby men of tomorrow.

The Hong Kong Union gave $15,000 to help finance early teams. Today, mini rugby spreads every year but the enthusiasts who give their time and knowledge to spread the game in Hong Kong would like to see it reach even more boys in schools and recreation clubs. Terry Orsler sees immense room for expansion among fleet-footed young Hong Kong Chinese to most of whom the world of rugby remains, unfortunately, very much a mystery.

Mini rugby, developed to help introduce the game to boys, is simply a scaled-down version of the game played round the world. There are smaller balls and smaller playing areas for smaller players. The nine-boy teams play games of 15 minutes a side for the under-ten groups and 20 minutes a side for the older boys. While the lore as well as the laws of rugby are passed on to the boys, the idea is not so much to indoctrinate the mini players in regulations of the game but to introduce them to the spirit of rugby. Good will, good sportsmanship, good fellowship. Skills are important. But fun is supreme.

Possession is still the name of the game.

1984

After their defeat by Australia the previous year, Fiji was coming back to Hong Kong in 1984 determined to give their traditional opponents a singing lesson. They intended to teach the Australians a few Fijian folk songs so the Aussies could join them in a victory chorus at the post-Tournament celebrations. The amiable giants from Fiji figured that they would be singing some songs of the islands that year instead of Waltzing Matilda. Others weren't too certain because the way things looked in the line-up announced by the Rugby Union, the winners of the 1984 Sevens could be singing anything from Land of Our Fathers to the Maori Farewell, the Marsellaise, Danny Boy or a Mandarin drinking tune favoured in the environs of Taipei. Because, somewhat to their own astonishment, to the hearty delight of the world's rugby lovers and the ecstasy of Hong Kong fans, the Sevens had taken another quantum leap forward.

Twenty four teams! The ninth Tournament was going to be double the size of the competition that had begun so uncertainly back in 1976. All the old favourites would be there, the battered faces of props who had for years been holding up scrums in Happy Valley and Sookunpoo, the

Opposite page: Protectively clutching the ball in one hand and fending off an attacking Tongan with the other, an American Eagle stands his ground.

veterans who had helped make the Sevens what they were. The plucky Singaporeans would be back, players who had never come close to victory but who never stopped trying. And the Koreans, seen by close observers as potential big winners one day not too distant. And the happy Solomon Islanders, the fiery Tongans, the doughty Japanese, the smiling Sri Lankans, the prancing highlanders from New Guinea and the jolly, banner-waving Bahrainis in their Arab headgear. Those monstrous, dangerously-fast Eagles were to be seen again at Sookunpoo and the slow-talking, swift-moving Canadians. Indonesia would be represented once more by an all-expat team of Dutch, French, Scots, Australians and English, a mini-UN rugby world of their own.

This Taipei player is about to hit the grass, downed by one of those determined Tongan tacklers.

Bottom: Teeth gritted with determination, a burly Korean speeds downfield away from an equally-single minded Hongkong pursuer.

Up she goes ... and up after it go French and Chinese players during the French Barbarians and Taipei match.

In addition to the familiar, there was going to be an infusion of new talent. France would send a Barbarian team and looking at the line-up announced from Paris it appeared they would be as formidable as anything Napoleon ever put into the field. The Wolfhounds from Ireland were heading for Hong Kong and their reputation gave rugby followers plenty on which to ponder. From Wales, a rugby nation second to none in its enthusiasm for the sport, came Crawshays Welsh and experts with memories of the feats of this team nodded wisely over the drinks in the Football Club bar and said this would be the lot to watch. But what about the other newcomers from Britain, the Public Schools Wanderers? They claimed they played for fun. But those who had seen them speeding down the field in successful tours that had taken them to three continents knew full well they also played to win. And that's what they confidently expected to do in Hong Kong. From Taiwan came Kwang Hua-Taipei and the Chinese team got an enormous hand from the crowd as they ran onto the field for their first game. They needed all the help they

could get because the luck of the draw had been cruel indeed to the Taipei team; they faced first the intimidating Australians and then the Canadians. Hong Kong had drawn a trifle more fortunately; first they faced Indonesia before New Zealand.

The All Blacks had once again come to Hong Kong seeking redress. For almost a century they had ruled the rugby fields of the world and be it Cardiff, Sydney or Johannesburg had trounced the mightiest foes that took the field against them. But in Hong Kong, their performances had ranged from mediocre to lacklustre to merely competent and although some of their foremost players had been included in their Sevens teams, it was the perceived wisdom of the experts that while the Kiwis were near-invincible at XVs, they could not produce a team that could play the very different, swifter, quick-thinking Sevens tactics. They were back to prove, once and for all, that the stadium professors were wrong.

The Hong Kong crowd was gleeful. With good reason. In addition to the new teams from countries which had never before competed in the Tournament, there was also a new trophy, the Bowl. The extra teams and the additional honour for which they would be striving meant an entirely new format. The 24 teams would be divided into eight pools. Elimination competitions would be held on the Saturday. Top of each pool would go into the Cup contest, second into the

Speedy Singaporean centre Frank Kwok nimbly dashes through the experienced Bahrain back line. Hong Kong's sister city to the South always sends a popular side to the Sevens. But then, so do the sand-lovers from the Gulf.

Plate and third-place getters would fight it out for the Bowl. The object was simple; to get every team into the second day's play and to give every player something for which they could realistically strive. Sri Lanka, no matter how hard they battled, despite all their efforts, could not really hope to overturn the Fijians. The Bowl was aimed at giving the less powerful, less experienced

teams, something they could aim to take home.
The new format, it was felt, would help foster the
long-held aim of the Sevens, to uphold and
improve rugby in the Asian-Pacific region. It
would also add to the excitement of the event. It
would also mean an entire Sunday devoted to
struggles for the three competitions. It would
mean more and better rugby for players as well as
spectators. And with the prospect of two dazzling
days of sport in front of them, Hong Kong rugby
followers scanned the sports pages eagerly
parleying reputations of teams and players,
rumours of prowess and ability, anecdotes of
talent and scoring strategies as they tried to
balance out the teams. As the end of March drew
closer, the new Union chairman, Glen Docherty,
anxiously kept an eye on the clouds. But even
quirky Mother Nature was on-side this year.
Saturday, March 31, dawned with a heavy dew, a
light wind, blue sky with fluffy clouds. It was
perfect Rugby weather. And over the next two
days the sun was to shine on what spectators
were to agree was as perfect rugby as one could
wish to see.

It was breathless, gripping, exciting. From the
second that leather pounded into leather and the
ball soared into air over the pampered grass of
Sookunpoo, there was never a mediocre moment.
The crowd roared and the hills were to echo with
approval, delight, dismay and rejoicing until the
final whistle on Sunday night.

The pool play worked well. The eternal battlers
scrambling for the bottom rungs of the rugby

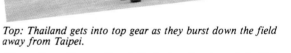

*Top: Thailand gets into top gear as they burst down the field
away from Taipei.*

*Above: Serge Blanco, French Barbarian star, is carried off the
field a wounded warrior. But even as attendants bear him away
to the medics, Blanco's eyes are still on the action.*

Next pages: A mighty tussle for the ball.

ladder had something concrete within their grasp,
and once knocked-out of the bruising contest for
the Cup and the Plate, there was sparkling play
by teams like Thailand and Kwang-Hua for the
Bowl. the Bowl was won, deservedly, everyone
felt, by Sri Lanka, a team that had been dutifully
coming to Hong Kong every year, doing their
best, being tackled by enormous Australians and
Canadians, being outrun by speedy Fijians,
dazzled by relentless Tongans but always trying,
trying, trying... but never winning. They got a big
hand when they collected the Bowl and the new
format was also roundly cheered for making the
Tournament fairer. But before the knock-out
competitions began on the Sunday, the Sevens
were to go through a shock as traumatic as any
experienced in the history of the competition. In
their pool, Australia were to meet the lively and

engaging Canadians, perennial improvers. All expected to see Canada give a good account of themselves before being dispatched by the Australians. But, as often happens in unpredictable Sevens play, it didn't quite work out like that. At game end, the scores stood at 10-10. There was discussion in the stands and in the officials' rooms. What team had scored how many tries? Under the rules, which one of them was on top? This was a question of vital importance because it meant one team would be going into the Cup competition and the other would be relegated to play for the Plate. But which one went where? The rule books were consulted. Points were tallied. Barrack room lawyers in the crowd argued judiciously over their jugs of beer and wine. Heads were scratched. On the stands, nobody knew what was happening and from what the spectators could gather, nobody on the field knew, either. Finally, it was announced the winner would be decided in accordance with the rules of the Tournament...on the toss of a coin! Up went the silver dollar and when it came down, the Canucks had called a head and went into the Cup. The distraught Aussies had been knocked out, not by better play, but by a stroke of luck, and the long years of the jeering "C'mon the convicts" cries were forgotten as the crowd clapped them off the field. It was a cruel twist of fate for the three-time winners to be dismissed from the main competition. Next day, they went on to win the Plate in true championship style and got well deserved applause for their sportsmanship.

A Fijian player is up-ended in the struggle for supremacy.

With Australia out of the running, the Wolfhounds soon put paid to any idea the Canadians may have had that they could proceed further in the race for the Cup. As the day wore on, with three knock-out contests for Bowl, Plate and Cup going on at the same time, there was a surfeit of excitement. One of the best matches of the weekend was between sparkling Fiji and dashing Samoa. The Fijians won 20-6. Then the Kiwis stormed to a 22-0 victory over the French. The Cup battle was drawing to an inexorable contest as Fiji knocked out the Public Schools Wanderers 12-4 and the All Blacks dismissed the Irishmen 12-10 in another stunning game. There was scarcely an occupied seat in the stadium for the last hour of the magical Sevens. Almost all 20,000 spectators were standing, cheering, clapping, stamping, as thrill topped thrill. The Bowl championship was at 5pm and Thailand and Sri Lanka gave a crowd-pleasing finale to the welcome new contest. Then Australia and Japan clashed for the Plate in a game that gave yet another unexpected measure of tension and drama with the Tokyo team scoring 20 points to the Aussies 26. It was a high-scoring game that see-sawed down the field and left the crowd hoarse.

But the Cup final! All Black officials were breathless in awe and astonishment. So was the crowd. In the entire history of world rugby, XVs or Sevens, possibly no display had ever been seen like it; the Fijians literally exploded onto the field. They put on a ballet performance in which skill, ability, flair and speed combined into a mixture that could not be equalled. The Kiwis couldn't touch them. the final score was 26-0 and, it was observed, it was a fair result.

"How can you beat that?" asked one awed New Zealand supporter. Even the Fijians popular manager, Ian Duncan, was almost speechless with wonder. "I've never seen rugby like it," he whispered. Nor had anyone else. Magic, uttered the sated fans. Bloody brilliant, said the Aussies on the sidelines. Mercury, said Kiwi coach Bryce Rope.

There was no doubt that the Fijians, four times winners of the Sevens, were the best team in the world. And at the farewell ball that night, Aussies, Kiwis and rugby players from all around the world learned a few words of Fijian victory songs. The men from the islands had already given them an unforgettable lesson in how to play rugby. Now as promised, they were teaching them to sing some Island melodies.

Competitions — 1984

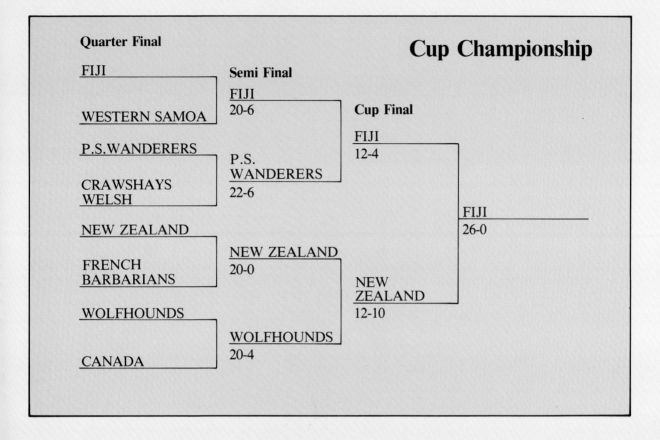

Cup Championship

Quarter Final

FIJI

WESTERN SAMOA

P.S.WANDERERS

CRAWSHAYS WELSH

NEW ZEALAND

FRENCH BARBARIANS

WOLFHOUNDS

CANADA

Semi Final

FIJI
20-6

P.S. WANDERERS
22-6

NEW ZEALAND
20-0

WOLFHOUNDS
20-4

Cup Final

FIJI
12-4

NEW ZEALAND
12-10

FIJI
26-0

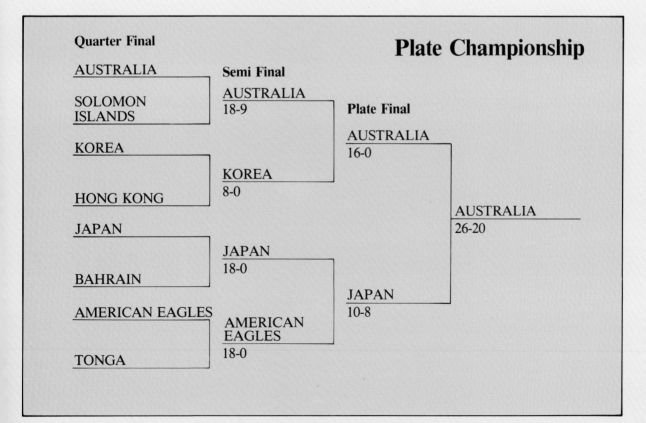

Plate Championship

Quarter Final

AUSTRALIA

SOLOMON ISLANDS

KOREA

HONG KONG

JAPAN

BAHRAIN

AMERICAN EAGLES

TONGA

Semi Final

AUSTRALIA
18-9

KOREA
8-0

JAPAN
18-0

AMERICAN EAGLES
18-0

Plate Final

AUSTRALIA
16-0

JAPAN
10-8

AUSTRALIA
26-20

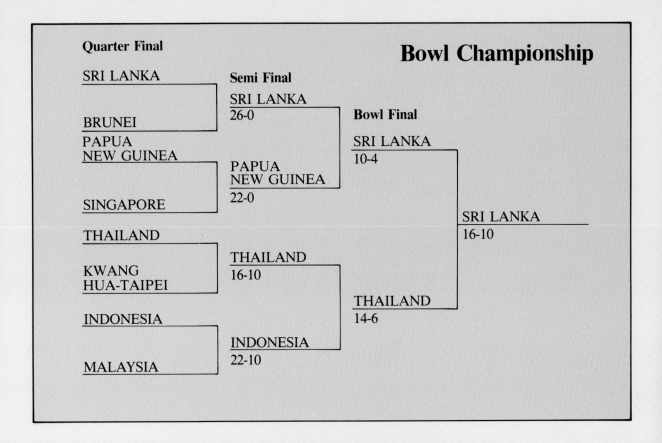

Bowl Championship

Quarter Final

SRI LANKA

BRUNEI

PAPUA NEW GUINEA

SINGAPORE

THAILAND

KWANG HUA-TAIPEI

INDONESIA

MALAYSIA

Semi Final

SRI LANKA 26-0

PAPUA NEW GUINEA 22-0

THAILAND 16-10

INDONESIA 22-10

Bowl Final

SRI LANKA 10-4

THAILAND 14-6

SRI LANKA 16-10

Players — 1984

American Eagles
Blane Warhurst
Mark Deaton
G. Detzler
Gary Lambert
J. Gehr
John Fowler
David Bateman
Steve Gray
D. Genkinson
Denis Shangagher (M)

Australia
John Maxwell
David Campese
Glen Ella
Mark Ella
Peter Lucas
Michael Lynagh
Brendan Moon
Gary Pearse
Chris Roche
Jules Guerassimoff (M)

Bahrain
P. Whittle
Colin Rick
Timothey Murley
Stuart Fluker
Andy Stevens
Mike Stapleton
Mark Thompson
Mark Moss
Bruce Collins

Brunei
Simon Moseley
Kenneth Swift
D.R. Johns
Tony Yong
Kadn Hamid
Sharbini H.J. Batiang
Aji Bin Hussin
Mark Card
Abdul Razak
John Williams (M)

Canada
Andrew Bibby
Ro Hindson
Anthony McGann
Pat Palmer
Roy Radu
Brian Spanton
David Speirs
Ian Stuart
Mark Wyatt
Monty Heald (M)

Crawshay's Welsh
Mark Davies
Kevin Hopkins
Paul Turner
Ieuan Evans
Colin Hillman
Kevin Bowring
Phillip Davies
David Richards
Robert Jones
Neville Walsh (M)

Fiji
Aliposo Waqaliti
Senivalati Laulau
Dominiko Manaseitava
Keleto Laboilagi
Acura Niuqila
Peni Rauluni
Etnate Gusuivalu
Panlo Nawalu
Sela Gutgutuwai
Ian Duncan (M)

French Barbarians
Marc Andrieu
Serge Blanco
Didier Codourniou
Patrick Esteve
Pierre Lacans
Patrice Lagisquet
Laurent Pardo
Philippe Dintrans
Philippe Sella
Jacques Fouroux (M)

Hong Kong
Bruce Vogel
Tim Lovell
Richard Pearson
Graeme Robertson
Alan McCullloch
Brian Eastgate
Ian Duguid
Eamonn McManus
Mike Bracher
Gus Cunningham (M)

Indonesia
Bernard Sherriff
John Smith
Alastair Speirs
P. Gia
Peter Merrett
M. Devooght
Christopher Andrews
Alain Pierre Mignon
S. Simpson
R. Horridge
David Thomas (M)

Japan
Seiji Hirao
Fukumi Kanaya
Kazuhiko Honjo
Yuji Matsuo
Yoshimitsu Koshiyama
Tsuyoshi Fujita
Hikaru Kawachi
Michihito Chida
Yoshimitsu Konishi
Hitoshi Oka (M)

Korea
Min Jun-Ki
Han Dong-Ho
Moon Young-Chen
Jung Hyung-Suk
Kim Hyun
Jung Keun-Young
Kang Chud-Sung
Hwang Ho-Sub
Cho Sung-Chul
Sohn Du-Ohk (M)

Kwang-hua — Taipei
Chern You-Tson
Chen Chi-Cheng
Pan Song-Pong
Yu Ching-Long
Jeng Wen-Jang
Chern Liang-Gan
Kao Hung-Chen
Chen Hsin-Yi
Chang Ging-Taring
Chen Po-Chuan (M)

Malaysia
Huzir Mohamed
Boon Hoon Chee
Lim Say Tee
Chong Chan Kiang
Roslan Siru
Yassin Saicl
Tan Ewe Hock
Resly Mayid
Zulklipli Aziz
Pang Kong Ying (M)

New Zealand
Wayne Smith
Allan Lindsay
Tony Thorpe
Richard Fry
Glenn Rich
John Kirwan
Mike Clamp
John Mills
Tony Lewis
Bryce Rope (M)

Papua New Guinea
Soiat Williams
Martin Bingeding
Herbert Peters
Emmanual Tobo
Innocent Oksen
Jack Takavis
Martin Taumu
Sime Ive
Paiwa Bogela

Public Schools Wanderers
Michael Harrison
David Cooke
David Johnston
Andy Simpson
Andy Ripley
Eric Paxton
David Bishop
Huw Davies
Roger Baird
Brigadier Rolph James (M)

Singapore
Chee Kum Thong
Henry Lee
Frank Kwok
Safri Kasim
Chung Hung Kee
Alan Wee
Mohd Rashid
Lim Khoon Huat
David Quek
Ishak B. Hassan

Solomon Islands
B. Eniti
John Bainivalu
Tele Delaverata
Wilson Ne'e
Fa'ako Liolea
Tigi
Billy Charlton Aluta
Peter Sa'atai
Josiah Tetia
George Kuper

Sri Lanka
Hisham Abdeen
Chula Dharmadasa
Chris Abeygunawardena
Len de Silva
R.T. Pieris
H. Rayan
Nalan de Silva
Saman Jayasingha
Shan Perera
A.J. Ratnam (M)

Thailand
Suvit Lamsam
Songsak Malithong
Chanwit Thongplub
Cheiw Chan Ruddit
Chucheep Kumfung
Yusuffi Aimwatana
Somsak Phnekpan
Pipat Nakpuang
Aroon Saenkosik (M)

Tonga
Otenili Pifeleti
Tuikolovatn Halafihi
Simione Tivi
Funa Moala
Pule Moala
Talai Fifita
Takai Makisi
Viliami Maka
Sweet Leilani Mafi
Sataki Tuitaveke (M)

Western Samoa
Taufusi Salesa
Sepe Tupuola
Tai Fong
Lomitusi Sasi
Tini Vaega
Pati Maligi
Dickie Tafua
Lolani Koko
N. Palamo
Paul Wallwork (M)

Wolfhounds
Jean-Francois Gourdan
Les Cusworth
Brendan Mullin
P. Power
Paul Dean
Michael Gibson
John Cantrell
Tony Doyle
Michael Kiernan
Karl Mullen (M)

Organisers

The warning by Ian Gow that more planning would be needed for future Sevens tournaments, if they were going to take place, soon proved to be only too accurate. The generous Sponsors who had been with the event from the beginning came back with promises of more support and as Union planners began preliminary talks about the games for the next year, they came up against a problem that nobody had foreseen. It was the problem of popularity, the two-edged curse of fame. Two scant years earlier, struggling against entrenched opposition from traditionalists to get the Sevens off the ground, this was a likelihood that had never been considered. If anyone in those early days had told Mike Pratt, Denis Evans, Brian Wigley, Tokkie Smith or Jack Johnston that they would be embarrassed by unpresented success, they would have laughed in scorn or cried in frustration. But there it was, virtually every day the mails brought proof of the stupendous success of the Sevens. This very success brought problems. More teams from more countries wanted to come. The Hong Kong Spring festival of champagne football had grabbed the attention of the rugby world with the effect of a tackle by a determined Welsh forward.

What should the answer be to this innundation of requests for invitations? It was not a matter solely for the organisers. More players meant more aircraft seats, more hotel beds, more games. And more money. Would the Sponsors agree to increase their already-magnanimous budget? Yes, said the companies that put up the finance. They would dig deeper to keep the event going. But could the Union handle anything larger than the one-day events? Could a group which comprised, essentially, enthusiastic amateurs provide the necessary back-up, the enormous managerial expertise, the assorted skills of entrepreneurs and organisers, caterers and promoters, needed to run such an expanded event? It would call for a very large degree of devotion from men who already had livings to make in diverse and demanding fields.

Tokkie Smith ran his own small import-export company. While being more or less his own boss, he still had to make a living. Mike Pratt worked for a Bank. Jack Johnston was a policeman. Denis Evans a consultant, John Stonham a doctor, Rod Allen an engineer, Malcolm Coates-White a computer expert, Glen Docherty an

Opposite page: In the officials' box, from right Ian Gow, Jock Campbell, Japan Rugby Union chairman Shiggy Konno and HKRFU president Gerry Forsgate watch play. To the rear, at right, is Tokkie Smith.

Chairmen of the Hongkong Rugby Football Union over the first 10 years of the Sevens gather proudly on the sideline during the 1985 tournament. Tokkie Smith (Right), Glen Docherty, Denis Evans and Jack Johnston have good reason to smile at the success of the event they all helped guide to renown.

Getting back into the swing of things, the four men who have been chairmen of the Hongkong Union over the first decade of the Sevens take the ball down the turf at the Football Club, the venue where the tournament was born.
At left, HKRFU president Gerry Forsgate waits for the ball as — from right — past chairmen Glen Docherty, Jack Johnston, Denis Evans and Tokkie Smith pass it out down an imaginary back line.

accountant. All were men of ability. But all had other, heavy career responsibilities. Could they, the Sponsors wondered, also shoulder the immense burden of running what was rapidly turning out to be a major international sporting event? Ian Gow and Jock Campbell had no doubt about the vision and capabilities of the men with whom they had worked so closely for the past two successful events, they just wondered if things were not getting too big to handle. This was a subject that the rugby men, too, had considered. But what they had achieved in the first two years had been such an outstanding success, had given so much joy to so many people from so many countries, that they felt compelled to keep going. Picking up the responsibility for the Tournament and running with it was as hard a task as any of them had ever faced on the rugby field. But it was one they felt they had to do. "Over the years, we had all of us got so much pleasure out of rugby that we felt this was an opportunity for us to put something back into the game," Mike Pratt summed up simply.

They may have been amateur entrepreneurs, but the item they were selling was much in demand by the public. Two weeks before the Tournament, tickets were selling rapidly. Those who had trouble getting into the ground the previous year were making certain that no such problems would recur. One happy feature was that the majority of tickets were being bought in 1978, when the Sevens were in the balance, in bunches of four and five; people were coming with groups of friends or with families, starting a tradition that persists. As the rains came down that year, the Organisers must have been grateful indeed that so many tickets had been sold in advance. They were also more than a little pround when the Guinnes Book of Records reached Hong Kong. The day it was put on sale, a rugby fan excitedly called Mike Pratt to tell him about a new entry in the book. It recorded the 1978 Sevens as the world's largest international rugby tournament. Not bad going for a bunch of amateur entrepreneurs. And so it went on into the years ahead ...

1985

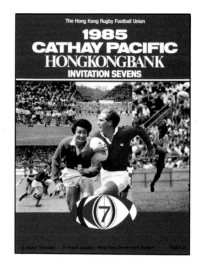

The weekend before the 1985 Sevens, Hong Kong fans were casting approving glances towards the heavens and talking about perfect rugby weather. But in the pre-dawn hours of Thursday as they lay dreaming about the glorious weekend before them, a sound not unlike that of the roar of the Stadium crowds woke them. It was the dull boom of thunder. And the radio weather forecasts held nothing but gloom. Thunderstorm warnings were being broadcast. And a late surge of the winter monsoon was bringing bands of cold wet weather a thousand miles deep down from China. On the pitch, officials and players watched the surface. It was in magnificent condition, thanks to the great work of the groundsmen. Followers of other sports had, sportingly, given the ground a rest for more than a week before the rugby and the grass was green, the markings were pristine white, the stands were swept and clean, the patrons and sponsors hoardings were gleaming and all that was needed to make conditions perfect was a hint of blue sky and a drying wind. Instead, the overcast continued to threaten and the wind was cold and damp. For the Kiwis, the seven Scots in the Public Schools Wanderers team and the

Welsh, the conditions were nostalgically like home, according to the jokes going around in the Hilton and on the playing pitches where teams were warming up. For the Fijians, Singaporeans, Thais, Sri Lankans and others from the balmy climes of the tropics, it was downright chilly. No matter. The thermometer may have registered a mere 11 degrees centigrade and on the pitch at Sookunpoo the wind-chill factor called for overcoats, but the players, officials and followers who had gathered from around the world were warmed by the thought that they were present to celebrate the 10th anniversary of the greatest rugby festival on earth.

Possibly no team were warmer than the Australians. They were practising at fever pitch. This year, if they failed to win, it would not be because a toss of a coin relegated them out of contention. This year, they vowed, they would not be put in a similar position to having their fate decided by a spinning one dollar coin because this year, you could bet the Sydney Harbour Bridge on it!, there were not going to be any draws. They were here to win every game from bursting go to all-out whoa. They were not

Previous page: Public Schools Wanderers get a brief spell with the ball. But not for long. A few seconds after this shot was taken Roger Baird came down to the mud and the Wallabies scooped up the ball. They showed that in Sevens, possession is the name of the game.

Below: An airborne Bahraini grabs what he can of a fleeing Tongan.

Seemingly alone on the field, Hong Kong winger Eammon McManus sprints down the pitch.

Next pages: Nimble All Blacks keep the ball moving as Brunei moves up to counter.

select and send national teams to Hong Kong because, simply, the Tournament was a world championship. The Welsh team, which was in effect a national side, was geared up for the weekend; they had been meeting regularly for practice sessions even before they left home. The Wanderers were not as confident about their chances as were the people they were likely to be playing. During a long and liquid celebration on the Wednesday before kickoff at one of Hong Kong's famous seafood restaurants on an outer island, their manager, Rolf James, summed up their hopes. "Not a chance," he said. But in the Sevens, anything can happen and over the beer before the first game it was generally conceded that anything probably would happen.

The North American teams both looked unpredictable but formidable. One of these years, the experts agreed, either Canada or the American Eagles were going to deliver a very sudden, rude shock to the more established rugby nations. The weight, skill and speed of the two teams were not underestimated by those most likely to be pitched against them. One year, either the Yanks or Canucks were going to suddenly click. Then they would storm right through the opposition. Everyone agreed on this. Was 1985 to be the year? And from North Asia, as well, there were dangers lurking for the unwary. Nobody was taking any long-odds bets against Korea or Japan being prominent, especially in the early games. Those likeable expatriate teams from the Gulf, Brunei and Indonesia were all sending their usual complement of Don Quixote's to tilt at the windmills of the mighty. But they couldn't really achieve much, could they? Could they?

And then there were the teams that the Tournament was really all about, the rugby players from Asia and the Pacific, the nations where fostering the love of rugby was the original intention of the Hong Kong Sevens. They were dispatching their best and brightest, swiftest and most talented players and although Sri Lanka and Thailand and Papua New Guinea and Kwang Hua-Taipei didn't really expect to topple the All Blacks or Ireland's Wolfhounds, they would certainly be taking to the field and doing their best. And while everyone cheered the Malaysian and Singaporean teams, there was in reality little hope of them battling past the Bowl competition. And what could you expect from tiny countries like the Solomon Islands? And Western Samoa?

Well, as it turned out, you could expect quite a lot. Quite a truly spectacular lot. Quite a

the only ones with this in mind. The Kiwis were of similar mind. Their manager, an amiable fellow named Bryce Rope, assured his countrymen at a gathering in the home of the New Zealand Commissioner on the Thursday night that his boys would be giving it all they had. What were the dangers, Bryce? Well, he mused over the cocktails in his slow Kiwi accent, he reckoned the big threat to the Big Three were the Public Schools Wanderers. This statement was to prove ruefully true. The Fijians, as usual, were not saying much. Their grins, wide as the Pacific horizons, said it all for them. The giants of Sevens rugby were not over-confident, they certainly were training hard, although rain persuaded them to cut out a Friday morning session, but their past record gave them justified confidence that they would be putting on a good show.

Much of the early speculation dwelt on the British teams. Crawshay's rollocking Welshmen were back and what a lovely bunch they were. Their leader, Kevin Bowring, put into words what many others had thought for years. Soon, he opined, the British rugby unions would have to

magnificent, stirring, blood-quickening, palm-jarring, throat-wrenching, pulse-raising, roaring, screaming, yelling, astonishing lot. Because Western Samoa, those gigantic elves, beat Fiji. It was a stunning, sudden, unexpected triumph. It was one of the great games of the weekend, one of the most thrilling games in the Tournament's entire history. The crowd couldn't believe it was happening, but there they went, the prancing Polynesians, literally running away from the mighty Fijians who for so long had so confidently worn the Sevens crown. With their typical open-hearted sportsmanship, the surprised, conquered monarchs congratulated the victors. The best team won, the Fijian manager, George Reade, said of the shock result.

But that was on the Sunday and on the first day of play it had seemed the Fijians were once again set for their customary glory. With the other big boys, they had romped into contention for the Cup. It was the lesser Plate placings that promised a grim tussle and the Bowl matches would be followed intently by the home supporters because Hong Kong, ingloriously, had gone down not only to the French Barbarians but also had managed to only scramble to a desperate

draw with a sprightly Indonesian side. The match of that first day was Australia and Tonga. The Aussies got a shock when the fiery Tongans stormed their defences and the 12-4 win for Australia was no disgrace for the Pacific Islanders.

As Glen Docherty noted early Sunday morning, men who came to the Sevens worshipped in many ways. After a cold and damp first day of the 1985 Sevens, they had been praying overnight for better weather. Somebody had obviously got the message through because the sky had cleared, the cloud had lifted, the temperature had risen a bit and although it was certainly not the sort of day to head for the beach to sunbathe, it was great rugby weather.

When the mini-rugby boys trotted onto the grass [which had held up much better than anyone could have hoped for] the stands were filling rapidly and crowds were streaming into the ground. They just kept on coming until a record 23,000 spectators jammed the stands to cheer,

The Public Schools Wanderers on attack.

Weaving, ducking, spinning, darting ... nobody could keep up with Australia's little wizard David Campese, seen in action against the Irish Wolfhounds.

jeer, shout with joy, moan with despair, leap with exultation and grimace in anticipation.

The Bowl competition saw a determined Hong Kong team take to the field with one aim in seven minds; to win. Thailand gave them a tussle but the home side won 14-6 then carried on to effortlessly cruise past Malaysia before crunching into a Papua New Guinea team that was equally determined to make its mark. It was a rousing, invigorating game and Hong Kong were lucky to scrape home 14-12. But they did well and the very skill and vigour they encountered on the field illustrated just how well the men who had a decade before planned the Tournament had succeeded in their task of raising the standard of rugby. Thailand, New Guinea, Sri Lanka, Kwang Hua... the standards of all the teams had improved dramatically over the years. The fact that Hong Kong had been forced to the limits to win was in itself proud proof the Hong Kong Sevens was successful in raising standards.

The Plate contests showed this same trend to an even more exciting degree. The luck of the pools now pitted Canada against the Eagles and many would have liked to have seen two teams with such similar strengths pitted against the lighter, swifter skills of wily Pacific or streaking

The enormous arms of the gigantic Canadian, Ro Hinson, seem ready to envelope a game Malaysian.

Asian sides. The big men clashed like mammoths and the Americans went on to face Bahrain in a cliffhanger that saw the Gulf side win 10-8. Tonga, still revelling in the shock they had handed the Australians, dispatched South Korea [another dramatically improving side] and then Japan before facing Bahrain. The crowd was split. Both sides over the years had built up loyal followings and the Arab headwear and the exhuberance of their followers in the stands matched the Bahraini style on the field. But nothing could match the fire in the Tongans bellies and with brilliant passing and the speed of attacking sharks they sped to a hectic, scrambling victory.

Fiji had loped confidently onto the field. They had reason to feel secure. In the nine previous

Sevens, they had won four times. They were the adored champions of the crowd and could expect more cheers to carry them to victory. But, suddenly, this scenario began to go disastrously wrong. It began as expected with a stylish Fijian try in the first minute. But then, the Fiji game plan fell apart. It happened so swiftly, so unexpectedly, that nobody could really believe what was happening. Slash, kick, run, dash... over the line went the Samoans. Then again. Now the crowd were cheering, bellowing approval for a magnificent, driving, brilliant offensive, just the same sort of scintillating play the Sookunpoo crowd had come to expect over the years from the Fijians. But this year, it was coming from the warriors from Western Samoa. All the world loves an underdog and this year the crowd had found new ones in the Samoans who notched up a 13-4 win over the champions. The Wanderers sent down the French, the Kiwis disposed of the Welsh and Australia bade farewell to the Wolfhounds.

If the crowd were lusty in their cheers for Samoa against Fiji, the tonsils took an almost unbearable beating in the semi-finals. Western Samoa streaked, magnificently, incredibly, to an 8-0 lead over the mighty Australians. But back fought the Wallabies and the sheer skill, the utter professionalism and knowledge of the Australians gradually edged them equal to the Samoans, then, inexorably, ahead to a 14-8 win. But it had given the men from Down Under a big shock — their second of the Tournament — and made the Cup final look a very even thing. It was to be a clash between giants, but not quite the giants people would have expected. As wily Bryce Rope had predicted on Thursday night, it was the Public Schools Wanderers who could pose a danger. They certainly proved this true in their clash with the Kiwis. The sides were even, but the Schoolboys had the edge and it was they who were giving the lessons to the All Blacks, who for so long had been instructing the world how to play rugby. The Wanderers, when the whistle went, had a convincing 14-10 victory.

And so onto the field came 14 men seeking to pronounce Sevens supremacy. In the stands, the lion of Scotland waved and a Union Jack circled the ground. But also in the stands, that doughty kangaroo symbol wearing boxing gloves and ready to do battle also fluttered from banners and the huge Aussie contingent were in full, wildly enthusiastic cry. What a game! That's what people were to say afterwards. What a great, thrilling game. And what a fillip for the

Mud-smeared but victorious, Australian captain Roger Gould holds the cup aloft. The win gave them four out of 10 championships in the first decade of the Sevens.

Hong Kong crowd that the ace Australian player was a Hong Kong boy, Peter Lucas, who had gone to school in the Territory and been capped nine times for the Colony. Oh, but what a game. The Wanderers made a beeline for the goal line to score. Then Lucas evened. Then an invincible Wallabies defence, an iron curtain of solid, mobile muscle, stopped the Scots in their tracks. To shouts of delight, the players clashed, crashed, kicked, ran, passed, whirled and spun through the mud in a thrilling Cup final that had the crowd on its feet. Australia! Come ON, Australia, roared their supporters. And on they came. And on. It was a decisive 24-10 win. You couldn't complain being beaten by a team like that, the Wanderers manager said. Nobody was complaining. Least of all the crowd. As they streamed home, or on to after-games celebrations, they could well be happy because no matter what side they had favoured, the 23,000 spectators had just seen one of the greatest days of rugby since the ball was picked up at Rugby School 162 years earlier.

The Aussies had said they were not going to be beaten this year by the toss of a Hong Kong dollar. They had shown that they weren't going to be beaten by anything.

Competitions — 1985

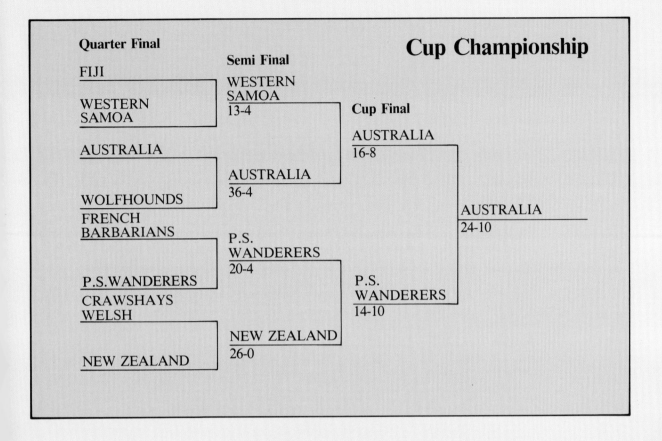

Cup Championship

Quarter Final

FIJI

WESTERN SAMOA

AUSTRALIA

WOLFHOUNDS

FRENCH BARBARIANS

P.S.WANDERERS

CRAWSHAYS WELSH

NEW ZEALAND

Semi Final

WESTERN SAMOA
13-4

AUSTRALIA
36-4

P.S. WANDERERS
20-4

NEW ZEALAND
26-0

Cup Final

AUSTRALIA
16-8

P.S. WANDERERS
14-10

AUSTRALIA
24-10

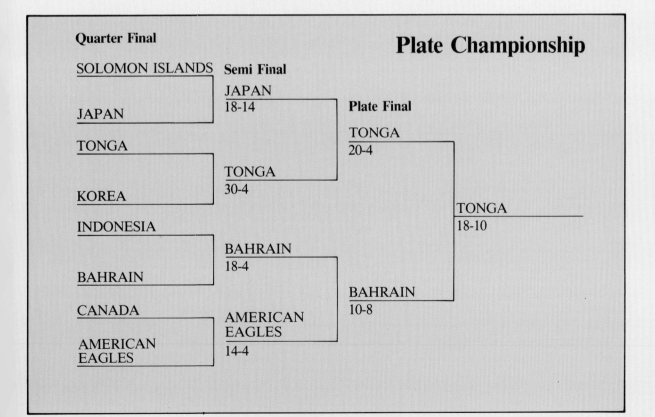

Plate Championship

Quarter Final

SOLOMON ISLANDS

JAPAN

TONGA

KOREA

INDONESIA

BAHRAIN

CANADA

AMERICAN EAGLES

Semi Final

JAPAN
18-14

TONGA
30-4

BAHRAIN
18-4

AMERICAN EAGLES
14-4

Plate Final

TONGA
20-4

BAHRAIN
10-8

TONGA
18-10

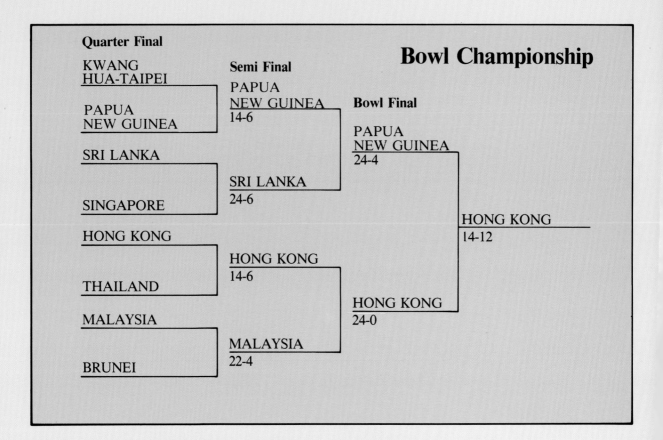

Quarter Final

KWANG HUA-TAIPEI

PAPUA NEW GUINEA

SRI LANKA

SINGAPORE

HONG KONG

THAILAND

MALAYSIA

BRUNEI

Semi Final

PAPUA NEW GUINEA 14-6

SRI LANKA 24-6

HONG KONG 14-6

MALAYSIA 22-4

Bowl Final

PAPUA NEW GUINEA 24-4

HONG KONG 24-0

HONG KONG 14-12

Players — 1985

American Eagles
Steve Gray
Blane Warhurst
Gary Lambert
J. Burkhardt
David Bateman
Terrence Titus
Charles Wilkinson
Dennis Shanagher
William Jefferson
Bob Jones (M)

Australia
Roger Gould
David Campese
Phillip Cox
Glen Ella
Bruce Frame
Peter Lucas
Michael Lynagh
Simon Poidevin
Steve Tuynman
Alan Jones (M)

Bahrain
Richard Duck
Neil Payne
Mark Thomson
Roy Leask
Stuart Fluker
Greg Barlow
Tim Murley
Andy Stevens
Colin Rick
Jim Fitzsimons (M)

Brunei
Pg. Md. Tajuddin B Pg. Hj.
    Othman
Bryan Reynolds
Baxter Sibidol
Brian Richards
Martin Lee
Philip Riddle
Aji Bin Hussin
Pg. Jamaluddin Bin Pg.
    Rendah
Tim Anderson
Karl Howard
Brian Richards (M)

Canada
Ian Stuart
Mark Wyatt
Jim Donaldson
Robin Russell
Tony Godzeik
Pat Palmer
Ro Hindson
Steve Gray
Tom Woods
Monty Heald (M)

Crawshay's Welsh
Michael Budd
Jeff Heardman
Terry Charles
Tony Swift
Clive Rees
Ged Glynn
Ian George
Richard Griffiths
Owen Golding
Arthur Rees (M)

Fiji
Rupeni Ravonu
Senivalati Laulau
Pita Naruma
Semi Talawadua
Paulo Nawalu
Aliposo Waqaliti
Dominiko Manaseitava
Acura Niuqila
Etuate Gusuivalu
Sela Gutugutuwai
George Reade (M)

French Barbarians
Daniel Dubroca
Eric Champ
Laurent Cabannes
Bernard Delbreil
Henri Sanz
Patrick Bonal
Pierre Chadebech
Jerome Bianchi
Pascal Jehl
Fernand Cazenave (M)

Hong Kong
Hamish Flett
Eamonn McManus
David Evans
Richard Pearson
Peter Evans
David Wilkinson
Gareth Parry
Tim Lovell
Brian Clesham
Gus Cunningham (M)

Indonesia
Steve Simpson
M. Betts
Henri Houllevigue
Alistair Speirs
M. Seward
Lennox Batten
Peter Merrett
W. Roxborough
S. Smeenk
Bernard Sherriff (M)

Japan
Michihito Chida
Masahiko Koshiyama
Shinji Onuki
Yoshimitsu Konishi
Kazuhiko Honjo
Seiji Hirao
Toshiro Yoshino
Masato Tsuchida
Yasuharu Kawase
Hitoshi Oka (M)

Korea
Jeong Jang-Kil
Ahn Deuk-khun
Song Youn-Ho
Kim Yeon-Ki
Kim Jang-Hyun
Kang Chul-Sung
Cho Sung-Chul
Lee Yoon-Seon
Choi Mu-roung
Shon Du-Ohk (M)

Kwang-hua — Taipei
Chern You-Tsuen
Lii Jenn-Fuh
Chen Chi-Cheng
Tsai Shou-Pou
Tu Shang-Fu
Yuan Ko-Cheng
Ma Na-Hsi
Ho Chih-Hung
Mae Chyan-Shuenn
Chen Po-Chuan (M)

Malaysia
Lee Kyuk Fah
Chong Chan Kiang
Ong Sing Chye
Sunsubaha Baharuddin
Abdul Ghafar Rajab
Ruslan Siru
Raja Omar Ikram
Mohd Muzamer Abdul Latiff
Zaini Kabul
Nik Ahmad Azmi bin Nik
   Mohd Daud (M)

New Zealand
Wayne Smith
Frano Botica
Wayne Shelford
Lindsay Raki
Glenn Rich
John Kirwan
Mike Clamp
Alan Dawson
David Kirk
Bryce Rope (M)

Papua New Guinea
Kepas Wally
Martin Bingeding
Paiwa Bogela
Ame Mowagi
Mark Pious
Peter Sarea
Don Tore
Peter Klink
Sab Doiwa (M)

Public Schools Wanderers
Roger Baird
Peter Steven
John Jeffrey
Mark Brown
Eric Paxton
Bob Hogarth
Jonathon Davies
Gary Callander
John Rutherford
Brigadier Rolph James (M)

Singapore
Ahmad Ibrahim
Andrew Chin
Allen Wee
Teo Han Chua
Richard Vanderput
Tay Huai Eng
Ishak Hassan
Chee Kum Thong
Lim Chye Lai
Tan Cheow Kwang (M)

Solomon Islands
Job Tuhaika
Tela Delaiverata
Fred Tango
Wilson Ne'e
Bro Eramodo
Boby Ramo
Donald Bennet
Josaiah Titia
Peter Sa'atai
Brian Eniti (M)

Sri Lanka
Rohan Guneratne
Bharatha Hegoda
Chula Dharmadasa
Chris Abeygunawardena
Len de Silva
N.S.S. Cooray
Shan Perera
Roshan Perera
H.A. Premasiri
Ajit Abeyratne (M)

Thailand
Apisak Premosoontorn
Kunthon Prachuabmoh
Yousubfee Aimwathana
Sawat Paimmunat
Poj Laksanasompong
Tirapong Thavornwong
Somsak Phuekpan
Pongkasem Aiemprapai
Songsak Malithon
Madhana Lansaad (M)

Tonga
Paula Tupou
Feao Lavemai
Sosata Lausii Hopoate
Alamoni Liavaa
Soape Nuku
Pule Moala
Talai Fifita
Fetiaki Langi
Foukimoana Maafu
Otenici Tuipulotu (M)

Western Samoa
Taufusi Salesa
Sepulona Moananu
John Schuster
Joe Apelu
Aniotelea Aiolupo
Dickie Tafua
David Schuster
Lolani Koko
Pati Maligi
George Meredith (M)

Wolfhounds
Donal Spring
Neville Ridgeway
Robbie McGrath
Les Cusworth
Ian Burns
William Burns
Iain Paxton
Tony Swift
Barry Evans
Anthony Twomey (M)

Sponsors

Why do two major business corporations think it worthwhile to invest money in a venture such as a sporting carnival. What, to put it bluntly, do Cathay Pacific and the Hongkong and Shanghai Banking Corporation, hope to get out of the rugby Sevens? In strict dollars and cents terms, not a lot. Not immediately. The cash registers are not set ringing because grateful rugby followers dash happily from Sookunpoo to show their gratitude to the sponsors by booking seats on Cathay or to discuss overdrafts with their local Bank manager. But in the wider realm, both corporations believe that sponsorship of the Sevens does pay off, at least in the incredible amount of goodwill the event generates. There are other spin-offs as well, not least of which is the enormous publicity that the Sevens Tournament now reaps throughout the world. When a Japanese player tackles a Fijian on the 22 metre mark at the Government Stadium, millions of people are likely to see the image on Tokyo television. In the background, etched unconsciously on their memories, are the logos of Cathay Pacific and the Hongkong Bank. The direct benefits of this sort of gratuitous publicity are, of course, absolutely unknown. It is impossible, both corporations agree, to quantify direct commercial benefit from sponsorship. For Cathay Pacific, it could be a few dozen seats sold on an aircraft bringing people to the Sevens. It might even be a couple of hundred seats sold over the next several years to players, officials or press who received a complimentary seat and recall Cathay's legendary inflight service and reliability. For the Bank, it is even more difficult to assess what benefits are reaped from sponsorship.

But for both concerns, there is a gigantic payoff in yen, won, piasters, francs, baht, pounds, rupiahs and every other currency in every land where rugby is played. Hong Kong is the home of the Sevens. It is also the home of Cathay Pacific and the Hongkong Bank. Both companies are linked inextricably in the minds of millions of rugby players with the Tournament. The Sevens, both corporations feel, now ranks as Hong Kong's biggest and best-attended sporting event. As such, both feel it appropriate that Hong Kong's own airline and the Territory's leading international corporation should be involved with it. Both do business, directly or indirectly, wth every country that sends a team to the Sevens.

There is more to it, though, than just money. Bank chairman Michael Sandberg was asked during the 10th anniversary celebrations of the Tournament if it was true that his corporation sponsored the Sevens from a selfish point of view, simply because some senior bank executives loved rugby. No, he answered thoughtfully, no. That was not the case. Of course, some bankers played rugby. More liked it. But it was because the Tournament brought so much pleasure to so many people that the Bank was so keen on its long association with the event.

Both Cathay and the Bank are, in one way or another, linked with the convention business. And the Sevens, bringing as it does so many people from all over the world to Hong Kong, is rather like a business convention. Of course, the currency discussed is one of tries and kicks at goal and tackles rather than the more commercial

Opposite page: HKRFU president Gerry Forsgate (right) and Hongkong Bank chairman Michael Sandberg flank Australian captain John Maxwell as he proudly brandishes the cup in 1982. Cathay's chief executive Duncan Bluck looks on.

Patrons boxes are hard to get — there's a waiting list that will never be satisfied — and it is a festival day for those who flock to the Sevens.

type of business convention, but it is a considerable gathering of people and any such gathering generates business. Thus people who would not otherwise meet come to Hong Kong every Spring in very considerable numbers and, inevitably, business is done. Business is good for Hong Kong generally and what is good for Hong Kong is very good for the Territory's own airline and its biggest bank. There are millions of others, especially throughout Asia and the Pacific, people who would not normally watch or read about rugby, looking at television and their morning newspapers for details about the game. Once again, this is good for Hong Kong and what's good for Hong Kong is good for Cathay and the Bank. That's the serious business side of sponsorship.

There's more to it than that, of course. Rugby is one of the few sports that has a global appeal for English-speaking peoples everywhere. But it does not, as an amateur sport, normally attract sponsorship. The investment that went into the Sevens, even as recently as 1980 when the Bank first took up co-sponsorship, was comparatively modest. That investment has paid off spectacularly; in the past few years the Sevens has rocketed into the sporting super-star strata.

Business apart, the Sevens gives businessmen a chance to participate in a worthy cause. Bankers do not normally like to be seen as idealists, but musing on why his corporation helped support the Sevens, a Hongkong Bank executive said as he watched the 10th anniversary Sevens: "In a world where international sport is visibly sliding into the political arena, it is indeed refreshing for the Bank to sponsor a sporting event which remains worldwide in appeal, avowedly partisan, yet clearly non-political.

"It is all the more pleasing to see this happen in Hong Kong, a small place geographically but a big business centre where east meets west, north comes together with south, not only to make money, but to play a game like rugby."

Cathay Pacific's managing director, Peter Sutch, sees limited direct commercial benefit in standing behind the Sevens as well as ill-defined but enormous long-term gains in goodwill. For the 10th anniversary year of the Sevens, at least 3,000 followers flew into Kai Tak Airport. About half of these, Peter Sutch estimates, were on Cathay jets, rugby lovers coming in from Narita, Gatwick, Kingsford Smith and airports all over Southeast Asia. Selling seats to the Sevens is possibly the least important benefit. As he sees it,

the airline's involvement in the event means a close association in the minds of the public between the airline and sport as a whole. When people think sport, they think Cathay. So when a sporting team anywhere in the world thinks of heading to the Far East, the organisers tend to think of the sporting airline. And that is Cathay Pacific, the airline that sponsors the Hong Kong Sevens. Why the Sevens? Partly because it is a universal sport in Asia. Today, it is played in just about every country in Asia, not only the traditional heartlands such as Australia and New Zealand, but increasingly in other nations like Singapore, Thailand and Korea. This spread of rugby in the region is something that could not have been foreseen when Cathay started as one of the initial sponsors and when The Bank came to the sporting party a few years later. Sponsorship was then a commercial gamble. It is certainly one that has paid off, given the enormous global publicity that now focuses on the event.

But apart from the commercial benefits that accrue to the corporations behind the event, there is also the equally important concept of putting something of value back into the community from which a company makes its profits. This is a belief that is held strongly in Asia, particularly in Hong Kong. The Bank and the airline are delighted, all thoughts of profit aside, to be putting back into the Asian sporting world something as vital as the world's leading rugby tournament.

Although the Hilton Hotel is not an official sponsor of the Sevens, the event would not be the same without it. The Hilton is the rugby players' home from home during the Hong Kong Spring. The hotel is also one of the long list of corporate patrons which hire boxes in the stand. This money-raising endeavour was a desperate necessity in the early, threadbare days of the Tournament. In later years, when the money came rolling in and success was assured, the early backers who stood by the Hong Kong Rugby Football Union when they were needed, are given preference when patrons boxes are allocated. Just as well; at last count there were scores of companies in Hong Kong, throughout the Far East and scattered all over the world which had placed their corporate names on the list for a patron's box.

There are evidently hundreds of big name companies who think it worthwhile having their names spelt large on the terracing of the Hong Kong Government Stadium when the world gathers to watch rugby.

After Game Festivities

Beer plays almost as vital a part in rugby as the ball itself. So it has been since the earliest days of the game, so it remains today and, it is universally agreed, so it will be forever. When the final whistle goes and the players troop mud-covered, sweat-drenched and exhausted from the field, the amber fluid is the international elixir that lifts their spirits. It is toasted to the victors and compensation for the vanquished. Why beer? Well, rugby historians say, honest ale was the most common drink in Britain when the game was young and beer drinking travelled the world as rugby spread. Doctors will add that after a hard-running 80 minutes on the grass, players engaged in a full-length rugby duel are likely to have lost a lot of liquid and need to replenish their bodily fluids. What better way than with a glass or three of beer?

In Hong Kong, this tradition is vibrantly alive and very, very well indeed. The Sevens would not be the same without the beer that flows so freely in the stands, on the terraces, in the sponsors' and patrons' boxes and, after the teams have played their final games, in the changing rooms. The flood continues unabated in nearby Wanchai

and in hotels where the Sevens Army of followers are staying. Beer, glorious beer; by the time the official celebrations begin in earnest on Sunday night following the championships, Noah could float his ark on the tidal wave of ale. It has been said many times before, remarked on with some wonder by numerous visitors, that despite this remarkable liquid intake at the ground and surrounding venues that the crowd at the Sevens are never anything but jovial, well-mannered and good-humoured. True, some may reach a highly-entertaining level of enthusiasm and the barracking may become more exhuberant as the afternoon wears on and the teams of girls delivering brimming jugs of beer make sortie after sortie to take succour to tired and emotional fans. But the mood is invariably affable, happy and friendly. The beer breaks social barriers; everyone is congenial, all are united in the back-slapping comradeship of the game.

The Sevens celebrations begin before the first game. As Cathay jetliners bring to Hong Kong thousands of players, officials and supporters, a few drinks help those aboard relax as they

Previous page: Tongans give an island melody. The words might not mean much, but the message of good fellowship is plain.

Below: Dressed to kill and ready to relax, three players get into the spirit of things.
Inset: As the night wears on... (or off).

Above: Enthusiastic international applause greets one of the turns at the traditional after-tournament celebration in the Hilton Hotel's grand ballroom.

Inset: Australia is also noted for horse-racing.

preview the competition. Once on the ground, newcomers to Hong Kong tend to have a quick shower, change clothes and head with swift determination and a good thirst to that renowned centre of culture, the Hong Kong Island area of Wanchai, the suburb that has become famous as the world of Suzie Wong. The diversions they are likely to find there are harmless and safe. In some of the bars, topless waitresses sit in lonely splendour and watch in mystified wonder as their customers, large gentlemen from many lands, drink copious amounts of beer and discuss some bizarre and unknown pastime called rugby. The ladies are not accustomed to being so ignored. But in Hong Kong in the Spring, a young man's thoughts are likely to turn gently to rugby.

Away from Wanchai, numerous other celebrations are being held. Various diplomatic representatives hold functions for their visiting sportsmen. One of the most notable, now part of Sevens lore, is the big cocktail party at the home of the New Zealand Commissioner where a sizeable selection of the Colony's Kiwis gather to urge the All Blacks on to glory. Meanwhile, at the Hilton headquarters of the Sevens, the managers gather for a semi-formal dinner before the competition begins. This is a chance for senior rugby officials from throughout the world to get together for a sporting summit meeting. Politics are out; it is a comradely meal over good food, fine wines — and large amounts of beer.

But the celebration doesn't come until after the last try has been scored, the last goal kicked and the Bowl, Plate and Cup presented to the winners. Then the players, held on a disciplined short leash to ensure top performance on the field, can let their hair down. This, many observers feel, is what rugby is really all about. It's not so much the results of the games themselves that are vital, important though they may be. No, they muse on the long flights home, the deep, inner meaning of rugby in general and the Sevens in particular can be glimpsed at 3am on a Monday morning in the grand ballroom of the Hilton Hotel where a Korean, Australian, Welshman, Samoan and Thai, arms around each other and singing old rugby songs in a motley babel of tongues, join together in goodwill. The words of the songs may be mutually unintelligible, as some spectators have remarked, but the tune is likely to be the same. And the message of goodwill and good sportsmanship is clear to all. And that message of true sporting feeling that transcends all barriers of nationality is the true meaning of the Sevens.

The Future

When international team managers sit down every year for their annual pre-Sevens dinner in a discrete private room at the Hong Kong Hilton, the focus is not only on the two-day fiesta of football in front of them. They are also looking further ahead, into the future. What does that future hold for the Hong Kong Sevens? A lot, all agree. It's not a question of will the tournament continue. That's settled, long established. It's how the Sevens will progress down the road, building on the sound and solid foundations excavated with such arduous planning and strenuous effort. Will the 24-nation format remain the same? Should the round robin structure be changed so the points slaughter in the first matches are eliminated and the striving minnows of the rugby world, hard-battling sides like Malaysia and Thailand, be spared the annual indignity of going down 50 points or so in games with the man-eating sharks of the rugby ocean like Australia and Fiji? Should there be three days of matches? Perhaps the sevens could be improved if only national sides were asked to contend. Would it be better if those teams that stand no chance of ending up in the finals of Bowl, Plate or Cup were substituted by other, more powerful teams? Above all, the question that dominates all others at these deliberations is: What is best for rugby in the Asian-Pacific region? How can the Sevens best aid and develop the sport throughout the enormous swathe of the world's biggest continent, the expanse of the earth's greatest ocean? That was why the Sevens were born. That remains the prime concern of planners today.

Such matters were the topic of even more than normal concern as rugby officials met in Hong Kong for the 1985 Sevens. This marked an important milestone along the high road of rugby history because it was the 10th year the Sevens had been staged. Many felt that by passing the decade mark, the Sevens had really come of age, that the Tournament had proven itself. By 1985, it was not merely a fixture in rugby calendars but also a major event in the international sporting year. It had, in short, grown and developed to a far more significant extent than those early optimists in 1975 could ever have envisaged. How to keep up this progress, how to continue development of the Sevens without risking the flavour, the traditions, the friendly feel of the games was challenge. What had come about over the decade was the growth of an international sporting event which had the flavour of a village

festival. That, many felt, was what it was all about, the folk gathering of world rugby, the global extension of the friendly game that Fijians might recognise from their village games under the coconut palms and Englishmen from their weekend matches on country village greens.

Invitation Sevens

One thing was certain, however, as Hong Kong Rugby Football Union officials watched the '85 tournament: the Sevens was here to stay. It wasn't a question of planning for the next year, outgoing Union chairman Glen Docherty and his successor, Brian Stevenson, agreed. It was what form the tournament would take over the next 10 years. How would things develop for the second decade? Here, little was certain, both felt, apart from the agreed fact that the Sevens would be played in 1995. The format? Well, both men admitted, the 24-team structure had proved superb. But who could tell if it would be retained? Nobody could look into the future and while the present arrangement seemed just about right, pretty near perfect, it was impossible to vow that it would never be changed. The two-days of matches was another fact of Sevens life. But once again, who could look ahead 10 years and say this would never be altered? Why, they argued, just look back over your shoulder at 1975. Who then would have been foolish enough to state that the number of teams would double over the next decade? Nobody. Likewise, there would have been few people around 10 years before who could have predicted the Sevens in 1985 would have moved to the big stadium at Sookunpoo and would attract crowds of more than 23,000. What was certain, Brian Stevenson and Glen Docherty held, was that any changes would be examined very thoroughly, all possible dangers looked at closely, before the very successful recipe of the Sevens was amended.

Opposite page: The Hong Kong Government Stadium — home of the Hong Kong Sevens since 1981.

The way things were, both men felt, the weekend fixture with 24 teams, was just about right. It was hard to see how it could be changed for the better. Certainly, suggestions that some of the weaker teams of Asian and Pacific nations be replaced by more successful sides from other nations would not be considered. The Sevens was started with the proclaimed aim of uplifting the standard of rugby in Pacific and Asian nations and nothing would be done, ever, which altered that. But the quality of some teams invited to the event could be upgraded. Would it become a World Sevens championship? This was a suggestion made by many. It was a topic of hot discussion both in Hong Kong and, increasingly, overseas. No doubt places like Australia and England and Scotland and Japan could organise an international sevens tournament and, with their huge stadia and big sporting administrative organisations, stage a world series. But would this supplant the Hong Kong Sevens or supplement it? And how would the international rugby championships, just announced and plans still uncertain in early 1985, affect the Sevens? These were questions to which, as the Hong Kong Sevens entered their second decade, nobody could supply any definite answers.

The danger, as many followers both in Hong Kong and abroad saw it, was that any changes would lose the charm. What would the Sevens be like without the mini-rugby boys? And how could anyone suggest the game Thais, the striving Malaysians, the zesty Sri Lankans could possibly not be invited? Impossible. They were an integral part of the Tournament. No, any refinement that meant sacrificing old friends was just not on. No way.

But where do we go from here? That was the question much worried at, greatly discussed, long debated, that Union officials and other organisers and the sponsors talked about in the annual wrap-up meeting after the 1985 series. It was difficult to improve the structure of the Tournament. Impossible, of course as one person had suggested, to move it from Hong Kong. Unlikely to welcome additional teams to the roll call of 24 nations. Absolutely unthinkable to even consider not asking back the old faithfuls of the past decade. The real problem was how do you change success. The answer, at least for the immediate future years, was that you don't change it. You go with proven formulae that have developed into established traditions.

The annual Davids-vs-Goliaths games would continue. It had been suggested that the less famous sides be pooled in a separate competition so teams like Malaysia did not face certain drubbings and going down 48-0 to Australia. No thank you the Malaysians replied very definitely. They wanted to face the big boys. They wished to return home and boast, despite the size of their defeat, that they had carried the ball against the famous Fijians or the mighty All Blacks, no matter how crushing was the defeat marked up on the score board.

And so, it appears, that is the sort of mixture to which the rugby fans of the world can look forward. More of the same. Years more of that friendly, comradely, laughing, happy, exciting, exhuberant, fantastic sporting fixture that has changed the rugby calendar and given a fresh, boisterous breath of life to rugby not only in Asia and the Pacific but throughout the world. Another decade of the Hong Kong Sevens.

One thing is certain, the ball will be kicked off at the Hong Kong Sevens for years to come.

Patrons Since 1977

Asia Pacific Capital Corporation

Bank of Bermuda Ltd.
Ben Line Steamers Ltd.
Bermuda Trust (Far East) Ltd.

Carlingford Insurance Company Ltd.
Cathay Pacific Airways Ltd.
Cazenove and Company (Overseas)
Cement Aids International Ltd.
Central Engineers
Chartered Bank
Chase Manhattan Asia Ltd.
Citibank N.A.
Citicorp Capital Market Group
Clark International Marketing S.A.
Mr. T. Clydesdale
Compass Travel Ltd.
Mr. D.E. Connolly
Cyanamid (Far East) Ltd.

Dairy Farm Company Ltd.
David Bayliss Ltd.
DHL International Ltd.
Dodwell Hong Kong Ltd.
Doyle Dane Bernbach (HK) Ltd.
Duty Free Shoppers

Ekman Pacific Ltd.
Eric Cumine Associates
Esso H.K. Ltd.

Fidelity International Investment Management
    (HK) Ltd.
Flowco Sales & Services (HK) Ltd.
Franki Contractors Ltd.

Gammon Building & Construction Ltd.
Gammon (HK) Ltd.
Gilman & Co. Ltd.
Gilman Engineering Ltd.
Leslie Gordon Esq.
Green Island Cement Co. Ltd.
Mr. T.J. Gregory
Grindlay's Bank plc

Hambro Pacific Ltd.
Heineken
Henderson Baring Management Ltd.
Henry Boot — Gammon Joint Venture
Hilton International
Hoare Govett (Far East) Ltd.
Hong Kong Aircraft Engineering Co. Ltd.
Hongkong & Kowloon Wharf & Godown Co. Ltd.
Hongkong & Shanghai Banking Corporation
Hongkong Electric Holdings Ltd.
Hongkong Hilton
Hongkong Land Company Ltd.
Hutchison Whampoa Ltd.

Inchcape Far East Ltd.
Inchcape (Hong Kong) Ltd.

Jardine Fleming Holdings Ltd.
Jardine Matheson & Co. Ltd.
Jardine Matheson Insurance Co.
Jardine Sports Association
John D. Hutchison Group Ltd.

Kim Hall (Hong Kong) Ltd.

L & L Roberts
Laura Ashley
Leigh Roberts Shipbroking Ltd.
Lloyds Bank International Ltd.

Macao Gentlemen's Outing Association
Mandarin Publishers
Max Factor
Mr. K.S. McConnell
Mr. B.S. McElney
Mr. D.J.T. McKenzie
Meridian Advertising (HK) Ltd.
Midland Bank plc

National Westminster Bank plc
New Zealand Insurance Co. Ltd.
N.M. Rothchild & Sons (HK) Ltd.

Otis Elevator Co. (HK) Ltd.

P&O Travel Ltd.
Philipp Brothers Hong Kong Ltd.
Pioneer Quarries Hong Kong Ltd.

Ready Mixed Concrete (Hong Kong) Ltd.
Repromac Ltd.
Reuters Ltd.
Richard Ellis
RTV

Salen & Wicander (HK) Ltd.
San Miguel Brewery Ltd.
Schindler (Far East) Management Ltd.
Sedgwick Chartered Hong Kong Ltd.
Sigma Coating Ltd.
Siam-Scot Co. Ltd.
Singapore Cricket Club
Skypak International (HK) Ltd.
Mr. N.W. Speakman
Sperry Ltd.
Swire Bottlers Ltd.
Swire Pacific Offshore Ltd.
Swire Properties Ltd.

Union Insurance Society of Canton Ltd.
United States Lines Inc.

Wallem & Co. Ltd.
Wallem Services Ltd.
Walter Wright (H.K.) Ltd.
Wardley Ltd.
Westpac Finance Asia Ltd.
Wheelock Marden & Co.